HISTORY OF
GOLF

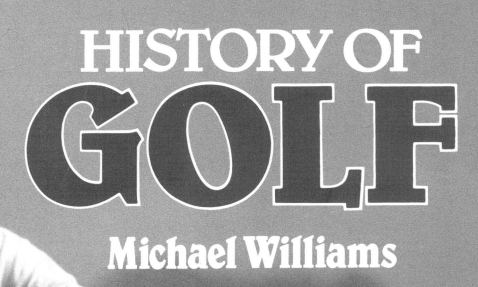

HISTORY OF GOLF

Michael Williams

CHARTWELL BOOKS, INC.

Dedication

To Judy who, without complaint,
kept the home fires burning

Photographic acknowledgments

Peter Adamson, St. Andrews (Royal and Ancient Golf Club) 14, 48, 49; Peter Adamson, St. Andrews 47, 132; All Sport, Morden 121; All Sport/David Cannon 106, 112, 134, 143, 147, 149 top; Associated Sports Photography, Leicester 33, 37 bottom, 38 top, 38 bottom, 65, 66–67, 68 top, 68 bottom, 69, 70 left, 85, 104 top, 105, 107 bottom, 116 bottom, 117, 135, 139; Australian High Commission 166–167; BBC Hulton Picture Library, London 23, 25 top, 34, 36 top, 44, 52, 53 top, 53 bottom, 54, 55 top, 55 bottom, 81, 101, 137; Bord Failte, Dublin, 160–161; Bridgeman Art Library, London 7; Peter Dazeley, London 2–3, 41, 89, 108, 127, 138, 140, 149 bottom, 150–151; Mary Evans Picture Library, London 10 top; Ladies' Golf Union, St. Andrews 20; Mansell Collection, London 8, 11, 16–17, 19, 79 left; Don Morley, Reigate 45, 71 bottom, 103, 104 bottom left, 104 bottom right; Muirfield Village Golf Club 158; David Muscroft, Sheffield 42 bottom, 86–87; H. W. Neale, Action Photos, London 6, 18 bottom, 21, 24, 25 bottom, 26, 30, 31 bottom, 37 top, 39 top, 40, 57 top, 59, 60, 61 top, 61 bottom, 62, 63 top, 84 top left, 84 top right, 84 bottom, 92 top left, 92 top right, 109, 115, 118, 119, 120 top, 131, 145; Northern Ireland Tourist Board 164; Peter Newark's Historical Pictures, Bath 10 bottom; M. Nuria Pastor, Barcelona 152; Photosource, London/Central Press 22 bottom, 36 bottom, 46–47, 50, 56 bottom, 63 bottom, 79 right, 82, 128, 144/Fox Photos 56 top, 64/Keystone Press Agency 15, 42 bottom, 57 bottom, 83, 87, 133; Popperfoto, London 13, 22 top, 31 top, 32 top, 32 bottom, 39 bottom, 51, 58 top, 58 bottom, 70 bottom right, 73, 86 bottom, 88, 92 bottom, 102, 116 top, 129, 130, 142; Royal & Ancient Golf Club, St. Andrews 18 top; St. Andrews University Photograph Collection 80; Phil Sheldon, Barnet 7, 27, 28–29, 35, 43, 70–71, 72, 74–75, 76, 77 top, 77 bottom, 78, 90–91, 93, 94–95, 96, 97, 98–99, 107 top, 110, 111, 113, 114, 120 bottom, 122–123, 125, 126, 136, 154–155, 156–157, 159, 162–163, 165, 168–169, 170–171, 172–173, 174–175, 176–177; South African Tourism Board 153

Front cover: Tom Watson USA (Bob Martin Creative Sport, Surrey)
Back cover: Augusta Golf Course, USA (Peter Dazeley, London)
Titlespread: Tom Watson and Jack Nicklaus, 1977 Open, Turnberry (Peter Dazeley, London)

This edition published 1985 by
Chartwell Books, Inc.
A division of Book Sales, Inc.
110 Enterprise Avenue
Secaucus, New Jersey 07094

Prepared by
Deans International Publishing
52–54 Southwark Street, London SE1 1UA
A division of The Hamlyn Publishing Group Limited
London · New York · Sydney · Toronto

Copyright © 1985 The Hamlyn Publishing Group Limited
Reprinted and updated 1986
ISBN 0-89009-737-2

Printed in Spain

CONTENTS

FOREWORD

A History of Golf is, by its very terms of reference, a daunting subject. Historians have for years been prowling through the archives with magnifying glasses, hunting clues that will throw a new light on some distant development of a game that, in one form or another, has been played for 500 years or more.

The greatest advance has nevertheless come in the last 100 years. The first Open championship was not born until 1860 and the United States Open did not follow until 1895. A golf course did not

Arnold Palmer looks up aghast as he thins a bunker shot through the green at Royal Birkdale during the 1961 British Open. His ball had moved as he was about to play. He declared the penalty stroke immediately but despite a seven at this 16th hole in the second round he still took the title for the first time.

even necessarily comprise 18 holes. There was no such thing as a steel-shafted club and golfers played in jackets, ties and stiff collars. Even the professional was still in his infancy and there was certainly no such thing as a tournament professional.

Such bears little relation to golf in the 1980s with multi-million pound and dollar circuits all over the world and, on big occasions such as the Open★, US Open and American Masters (itself not born until 1934), audiences of millions as television bounces the play live from satellite to satellite and thereby into the homes of many lands.

Prior to 1860 could therefore be termed as Ancient History; post 1860 as Modern History. There is of course no argument but that the two are related. However in this History of Golf, I have concerned myself mostly with the past 100 years. It was not until then that the seeds of the game were taken from Scotland and planted abroad. Nor was it until then that the great players started to become recognized as national sporting heroes.

Golf is a game about people. The mastery the champions have of hitting a ball of 1.68in (4.3cm) in diameter into a hole 4¼in (10.8cm) wide, through avenues of trees, round bunkers, up hill, down dale and over water for distances of up to 600 yd (540m) in an average of less than four strokes is a thing of wonder to the masses.

For that reason one chapter is devoted to 20 of the greatest players, from Harry Vardon, whose career spanned the years at the turn of the century, to Severiano

Ballesteros. The choice is a subjective one, as must be, too, the selection of 20 outstanding golf courses.

Golf is unique in that of the many hundreds of thousands of courses all over the world, no two are exactly the same. Some individual holes stand comparison and there have been attempts even to imitate. But it is almost impossible to reproduce to the last detail. The surroundings, terrain, turf, weather and just 'feel' of the place always differs.

Every course, therefore, offers a different challenge and to play well in one country does not necessarily guarantee similar success in another. Dr Cary Middlecoff, a US Open champion, once remarked that he always 'had difficulty in getting my game past the airport'. It was, therefore the ability of someone such as the South African Gary Player to be a champion in many lands that sets him and others apart.

Golf is fortunate in that it has become a game of traditions and for that reason the Open Championship, the US Open, Masters and the American PGA have a special place. These are the world's four 'majors' and it is right to give them due prominence. Their development over the years has had much to do with the game's expansion.

Because golf is a game in which referees play a very minor role, players are put 'on their honour' much more so than in some sports. It is the easiest game in which to cheat, for the golfer is often his only witness – and therefore his only judge.

When Arnold Palmer won the Open Championship at Royal Birkdale in 1961 he had a seven at one hole when there was not another person present who did not think other than it had been a six. As he prepared to recover from a bunker, Palmer's ball moved fractionally. Only he was aware of it, knowing too that it was a penalty stroke. He called it at once. But the gods have a habit of rewarding virtue. Palmer still won his first British Open, by a stroke.

There have been many such incidents over the years. Players constantly seek advice from one another about their swings and it is freely given, even if those self same golfers are in contention with one another for a major prize. When Tom Watson faced a short putt to win the Open Championship at Turnberry in 1977, it was Jack Nicklaus, having just sunk a huge putt that could have earned

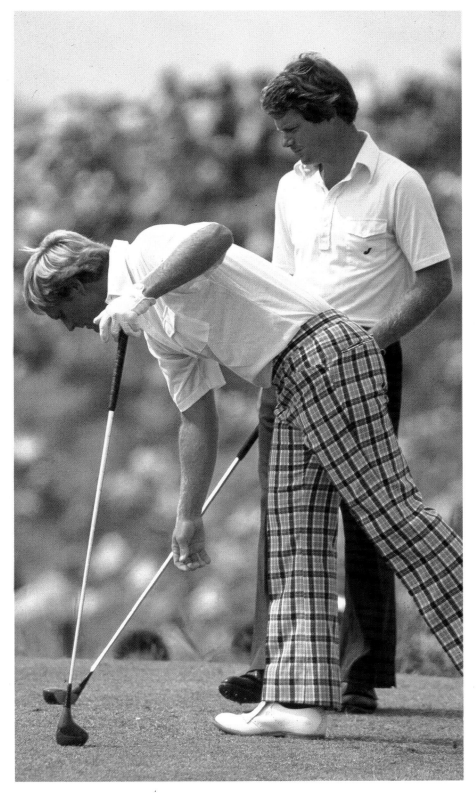

him a tie, who called the crowd to order so that his opponent be given a fair chance to beat him, which he did.

The code of conduct is high and rightly so, for there is an enchantment to golf that is somehow quite separate. It was captured by two lines from John Betjeman's *Seaside Golf*:

A glorious, sailing, bounding drive
That made me glad I was alive.
Michael Williams

*Throughout the book, the term 'the Open' refers to the British Open Championship unless otherwise indicated.

Jack Nicklaus, watched by Tom Watson, stoops to remove his tee peg after driving off in their epic confrontation in the 1977 British Open at Turnberry.

1 DEVELOPMENT OF THE GAME

Of all mankind's inventions, the one that has given the greatest pleasure has been the ball. Basically it can be dealt with in four ways. It can be thrown, caught, kicked and hit. It can also come in different sizes and even shapes, like the rugby ball, which is oval. With different balls came, in the fullness of time, various games. All of them began in some way and somewhere, though historians are still arguing as to how golf started and who, indeed, gave it to the world. It is commonly believed to have been the Scots, but there is a school of thought, and indeed some evidence, that in fact it was the Dutch who first started swatting a ball about with some sort of club. However, as some Flemish paintings depict the activity as taking place on ice, it could presumably have been the forerunner of ice hockey or even hockey, golf once rather disrespectfully having been described as 'hockey at the halt'.

No doubt historians would regard this as a rather flippant approach to a very serious matter. Indisputable evidence of golf can be found in the Scottish parliamentary statute books of the 1400s when 'the gouf', as it was then called, was banned by King James II of Scotland because it was becoming too popular a pastime interfering with archery practice, necessary for national defence in the periodic wars against England.

At least three such edicts were issued, indicating that golf in Scotland was popular, to say the least, and that the public was disinclined to listen to its lords and masters. Perhaps the turning point for the game in these Middle Ages was the fact that royalty subsequently took a liking to the game. In 1502, King James IV of Scotland acquired a set of clubs and balls from a bowmaker in Perth, while in 1567 Mary Queen of Scots was rebuked for playing golf at

An artist's impression of something resembling golf, dated 1384 and taken from a manuscript in the Douce Collection.

Winter landscape by the Dutch artist Willhelm Koolen, 1608–1666.

Seton House soon after the death of her husband, Darnley.

At about this time the Archbishop of St. Andrews had given permission to the community to play golf over the local links, though in 1592 there was a proclamation against it taking place at Leith during the time of the Sunday sermons. To this day the courses at St. Andrews are closed on the sabbath, other than by special dispensation such as the final round of the Open, which now ends on a Sunday.

There is no mention of golf in England until the 17th century when King James VI of Scotland ascended the throne as King James I of England and took his courtiers to Blackheath, then on the outskirts of London. There was also mention of the game being played at Tuttlefields, which subsequently became the playing fields of Westminster School, in Vincent Square, though always referred to by the boys as 'Up Fields'. Neither were likely to have been golf courses as such and the game did not really begin to take shape until the 18th century when the first Clubs and Societies were formed, the members meeting in the local hostelry, electing office-bearers, drawing up rules and putting up prizes.

In this context the Gentlemen Golfers of Leith (later to become the Honourable Company of Edinburgh Golfers) are credited as being the 'founders of the founders', competing in 1744 for a silver club presented by the City of Edinburgh. Certainly it was the Gentlemen of Leith who that year drew up the first Rules of Golf. There were only 13 of them, but they form the basis of the 34 in operation today.

Ten years later came the formation of the Society of St. Andrews Golfers, the membership gathering for much eating and drinking either at Baillie Glass's or the Black Bull Tavern. It was nevertheless not until 1834 that King William IV became the Society's patron and conferred the title of the Royal and Ancient Golf Club of St. Andrews.

Other Clubs and Societies soon followed and the first recorded competition at Blackheath, England's most senior club, took place in 1766. It had become a game for the well-to-do, having some association, it is thought, with the masonic movement with the players wearing long red coats and breeches.

9

An artist's impression of some early play at Leith, the home of the Gentlemen Golfers of Leith. They later became the Honourable Company of Edinburgh Golfers and were responsible for the first Rules of Golf, in 1744.

'The Golfers', a painting at St Andrews, 1847. No sign of crowd control in those days!

Carrying clubs was beneath them and among the duties of the caddies, with their armfuls of loose clubs, was to clear the course of an unenlightened public, frighten off the rabbits and retrieve the balls from holes that would ultimately become elbow deep. The teeing ground would be near to the previous hole, there being no such thing as a green.

In those early days there was no distinction between professionals and amateurs. The game was mostly played by foursomes, but by degrees the club- and ball-makers grew in expertise, not only as craftsmen but at the game itself. To augment their incomes, challenge matches were arranged and they drew big followings over the links of St.

10

Andrews, Prestwick, Musselburgh and North Berwick. Allan Robertson, a St. Andrean, was the best of them all and it was his death, in 1859, that vacated a throne that was only re-occupied with the arrival of the first official Open champion in 1860.

This event could in many ways be looked upon as the introduction of stroke-play as a form of competition. Hitherto it had been almost exclusively match-play. Nor were there any such things as golfing clothes. Until the First World War the now rapidly expanding game was contested by players in jackets and ties and everyday, smooth-soled shoes. It was the American, Walter Hagen, in the 1920s who changed all

that, introducing cardigans and pullovers in pastel shades, two-tone spiked shoes and altogether a sartorial elegance that set the fashion for the future. The tie was the last relic of the past to depart, Bobby Locke still wearing one in his Open championship-winning years of the 1950s.

As the British Empire expanded, so golf was taken to the far corners of the earth. Calcutta, now Royal Calcutta, is the oldest club in the world outside Britain. It was founded in 1829, while it was not until 1864 that England had its first links, at Westward Ho! in Devon.

The number of holes that constituted a round had nevertheless still to be standardized, it tending to vary from

One of the founder members of Royal Blackheath, the oldest club in England. There was no such thing as a bag for the caddie to carry his master's clubs in the 18th century.

between five and 12. St. Andrews once had 22 holes, but in 1858 the Royal and Ancient issued new rules to its members and the first of them stated that 'one round of the links, or 18 holes, is reckoned a match unless otherwise stated'. Prestwick was nevertheless still a 12-hole course when the Open was first played there in 1860.

The first continental Club was Pau, in France, in 1876, and the first in Australia, Royal Adelaide in 1871, the prefix coming later. Golf arrived on the North American continent through the officers of the Scottish trading ships with the birth of (Royal) Montreal in Canada in 1873 while in 1885 the (Royal) Cape Club was founded in South Africa. Though there are traces of the game before, it was the formation of the St. Andrews Club, in Yonkers, New York, in 1888 that is looked upon as the birthplace of the game in the United States.

Hong Kong, in 1889, saw the beginnings of the game in the Far East, soon followed by Thailand and Japan, where the first course was one of nine holes on the lower slopes of Mount Rokko, near Kobe. As the years passed, so the expansion continued to all parts of the globe and even beyond. It was in 1971 that Captain Alan Shepard, Commander of Apollo 14, hit two shots with a telescopic six iron on the moon. The Royal and Ancient at once sent a telegram reminding him that 'before leaving a bunker a player should carefully fill up and smooth over all holes and footprints made by him' failure to do so being a breach of the etiquette of the game!

Clubs and Balls

The development of the golf ball and the golf club are interwoven, for as improvements were made in one, so they had to be made in the other. William Mayne, who tooled bows and arrows, is the first acknowledged clubmaker, being appointed to the court of King James I of England, who took a liking to knocking a ball around. The ball of that time has since become known as the feathery, a hatful of boiled feathers being stuffed into a small leather pouch, stitched and then hammered until roughly round.

It was a long and laborious process, all done by hand so that not even the quickest worker could produce more than four or five a day. Consequently it was both expensive and harmful, since the inhalation of particles of feathers caused both asthma and lung disease.

The feathery was also subject to weather conditions; it grew heavier when wet, the stitching was inclined to break and, rarely being truly spherical, it was also unpredictable when putting. Its resilience on impact nevertheless meant that clubs did not have to be particularly strong; the shafts were made of hazel or ash and the heads, much longer and shallower than they are today, of blackthorn, beech, apple or pear.

Nevertheless the feathery lasted some 400 years until the mid 1800s when the gutta ball first appeared. It was made of gutta percha, from Malaya, and was a sort of elder brother to the gutty, a composite ball of gutta percha, ground cork, leather, metal filings and an adhesive liquid. The gutty came on to the market in about 1870 but it was the gutta that had provided the breakthrough, though in whose hands has never precisely been established. One popular tale is that the invention belonged to a Dr. R. Paterson, of St. Andrews, who discovered that the gum on the soles of his worn out shoes could be melted down and then rounded into a very acceptable golf ball.

This technological advance however did not immediately improve the standard of play. The gutty tended not to travel through the air as well as the feathery, especially when new. There was, though, a distinct improvement the older the ball became, due, it was discovered, to the scuffs and grazes the ball received. It is one of the principle's of aerodynamics that an uneven surface on a ball hit with backspin will send the air rushing over it with a consequent drop of air pressure and the relatively higher pressure beneath the ball forcing it up.

New gutties were therefore deliberately scored on manufacture by hammer and chisel, before indentations, or dimples, were proved to be even more effective. However, the harder ball did cause more wear and tear on clubs, leather insets having to be inserted in the faces. More resilient shafts were also necessary and hickory, from North America, was found to be the answer.

There was also an increase in the use of clubs with iron heads, the forerunners of today's irons. At first they were simply 'trouble' clubs, used for escaping from

hazards such as ruts in the ground. Allan Robertson was the first to master clubs like the mid iron, cleek, niblick and mashie, all of which became popular under his influence. However, by the late 1890s another change took place when an American dentist, Coburn Haskell, perfected the rubber-wound ball, comprising a small core of gutta percha wound with elastic thread and then encased in a shell of gutta percha.

The Haskell was found to fly another 20–30yd (18–27m), though at first it was regarded suspiciously by the professionals. However, in 1902 Alec Herd tried one in practice for the Open at Hoylake and was so impressed that he used it to win the championship itself. This success effectively signalled the end of the gutty after a reign of 50 years.

A change of ball again meant a change of club design and construction. A much harder wood was needed for the head to withstand constant impact and it came from persimmon, which, like hickory, was discovered in America. Demand soon began to exceed supply however and successful experiments were made with laminated, composition and, more

recently, metal heads. Further protection from the general wear and tear came with the use of brass sole plates and insets of bone, ivory and then, more economically, plastic.

Hickory was in short supply after the First World War, resulting in experiments with steel, which proved a big advance, the steel shaft being legalized in the United States in 1926 and in Britain in 1930. It was much more durable than hickory and mass production quickly brought the arrival of the matched set of clubs with graded shaft-lengths, lofted club-heads and all perfectly balanced. Such scientific perfection meant, in theory, a 10-yd (9m) difference in the distance of the shot from club to club, but the choice available meant that in the 1930s some players (or rather their caddies) were carrying as many as 25 clubs. Between them the Royal and Ancient (R & A) and the United States Golf Association (USGA) then moved in and limited the number to 14, which has remained the maximum ever since.

Fourteen clubs is still a sizeable number and the modern set now comprises three woods (usually the driver

Some old-time giants of the game at St. Andrews. Second left is Old Tom Morris, who won the British Open four times. Third from the right is Allan Robertson, the supreme golfer until his death in 1859, while on his right is young Jamie Anderson, who won the British Open three times in a row from 1877.

and the three and five woods), nine irons (from two to wedge), a sand iron and a putter. Some professionals tend to forfeit the five wood in favour of a one iron, which is a useful alternative for driving at holes with narrow fairways.

Housing this armoury has brought a marked increase in the size of golf bags, big enough to carry almost everything bar the kitchen sink. On the other hand, there has been a gradual decline in the number of caddies, leading to wider use of the golf trolley and the introduction of the electric cart, on which two people can ride with their bags strapped to the back. This is particularly useful in the hot countries and also to the more elderly,

who might otherwise not be able to continue playing. However these vehicles may not be used either by professionals or amateurs in major competition.

Since the Second World War, further improvements have sent the ball travelling much further than it did. To prevent golf courses becoming outdated, or too short, both the R & A and the USGA have imposed a velocity restriction which, under machine testing, is limited to 250ft (75m) per second, with a two per cent tolerance, in other words 255ft (76.5m) per second.

Extra distance now tends to be sought 'through the air' by subtle changes to the

Some early wooden clubs.

dimple configuration during manufacture. Surlyn was found to be a more durable cover for the average player, being more resistant to the mis-hit. But it is not favoured by the better players, who still prefer balata for the greater 'feel' and control they can get in their shot making. Similarly, the more recent two-piece solid ball, with its tough, synthetic cover and a hard, resilient core is more popular with those seeking durability and distance rather than finesse.

For many years one of the game's absurdities was that golf in America was played with a ball 1.68in (4.3cm) in diameter while Britain and much of the rest of the world used one of 1.62in (4.2cm) though both weighed 1.62oz (46 grammes). British manufacturers, having a monopoly of the smaller ball market, were particularly anxious to preserve it, but there was a minority of far-sighted people who recognized the virtue of the bigger ball as the more difficult to play but, once mastered, producing more capable golfers.

The first big-ball professional tournament in Britain was at Wentworth, Surrey, in 1960. There was a further, experimental 'one-off' season in 1964 and in 1968 it was introduced again, on a three-year basis. It has remained the tournament ball in Europe ever since though it was not until 1974 that it was made compulsory in the Open and not until the early 1980s that it came into play in the British Amateur championship. The various national, county and club competitions soon followed suit and sales of the small ball have now dropped to some five per cent. A major demarcation line in the game world-wide has therefore been breached.

Government of the game

From time to time some of the 400 or so different makes of golf ball may be declared illegal, as may be some clubs. Approval of new products or inventions is made by the R & A and the USGA who

A monorail track in Japan used for transporting sets of clubs round a course. Each unit holds four bags and is operated by push-button.

work closely together as the 'Government of the Game'. Authority was first thrust upon the R & A, a private club, when the Gentlemen Golfers of Leith, who had drawn up the original rules in 1744, suffered some internal wrangling. The R & A was subsequently regarded as the most senior body and when, towards the end of the 19th century, it became obvious that some sort of uniformity was needed, it was they who appointed the first Rules of Golf committee, in 1897.

America were meanwhile going their own way, the USGA, which was formed in 1894, conferring only occasionally and informally with the R & A. Indeed it was not until 1950 that the two bodies agreed on a uniform, world-wide code of rules, though even then they could not settle differences over the minimum size of the

ball. The two bodies now meet every four years to review the rules, which were completely reorganized and to some extent simplified as recently as 1984.

Changes are nevertheless made only after the fullest consultation with the 50 or so unions and associations, many from overseas, affiliated to the R & A. The Rules committee itself has repre-sentatives from the Council of National Golf Unions (England, Scotland, Wales and Ireland) Europe, Australia, New Zealand, Canada, South Africa, South America, Asia, the Pacific and the United States. In addition there is to be an International Golf Conference every four years beginning at St. Andrews in 1985, to which the British Professional Golfers' Association is also invited.

An artist's impression of the St. Andrews' caddies scrambling for the ball the new R & A captain (inset) has driven down the first fairway. The successful caddie receives a gold sovereign in return for the ball, which is then hung on a silver club.

Below: The members assemble in readiness for the new captain to drive himself into office at the Royal and Ancient. The ceremony is traditionally held during the club's autumn meeting.

One of the major duties of the committee is to clarify rules which are still sufficiently complicated to bring a constant stream of queries from all over the world. Consequently there is a 'decisions sub-committee' which in 1984 combined with the USGA in issuing a Joint Consolidated Decisions service on a world-wide basis.

The technological advances in the production of clubs and balls have resulted in the R & A setting up a special Implements and Balls committee, which also works in close harmony with the USGA, at whose headquarters at Far Hills, New Jersey, there is special testing equipment to ensure conformity with the specifications as laid down in the rules.

Right: Col. Tony Duncan (left) makes clear the rules to Jack Nicklaus during the world match-play championship at Wentworth in 1971. Nicklaus wanted a 'free drop' because an advertising hoarding between himself and the green could have interfered with his shot. Duncan refused and when he subsequently offered to stand down as referee, Nicklaus agreed. Gary Player won the match and title by five and four.

An artist's impression of a busy morning at the Westward Ho! and North Devon Ladies Club, dated around 1873. Only putting took place for it was considered unladylike to swing the club beyond shoulder height.

Another important function of the R & A concerns amateur status, particularly with the marked increase in commercial sponsorship. An Amateur Status committee was established in 1966 and, apart from periodic revision of the rules which limit prizes or vouchers in Britain to £150 and elsewhere to 350 dollars, a considerable amount of time is taken up with requests for reinstatement of amateur status. Principally these come from young players who turn professional too soon. Reinstatement is invariably granted, but only after a suitable interval governed by the applicant's length of professional service.

The focal point of the R & A, from the public's point of view, is nevertheless the Open championship. It has been run by the club's Championship committee since 1919 and, apart from a professional secretariat, the committee consists exclusively of club members. Club membership is by invitation only, now 1,800 strong, 750 from overseas.

Open championship costs now run at around £1.5 million, though television and film rights have helped to create a surplus and this, in turn, is used to fund such as the Amateur championship, the Youths', the Boys' and the Seniors' championships and also amateur international matches involving British teams both at home and abroad.

Further substantial contributions are made by the R & A to other golfing bodies to foster the development of the game; in 1985 for example, they came to the rescue of the Ladies Golf Union, putting up the prize money for the British Women's Open, which was in danger of disappearing after commercial sponsorship had been lost.

Ladies to the fore

Although there had been earlier references to women playing golf, notably among the fisherwives at Musselburgh, they did not really get a foothold in Britain until 1868 with the formation of the Westward Ho! and North Devon Ladies Club, which had its own nine-hole course. Play was limited to alternate Saturdays between the beginning of May and the end of October and to use of the putter only. Vigorous exercise was not approved, though the fashions of the time made a full swing impossible.

However it was not long before other Clubs began to spring up. The London Scottish Ladies was formed in 1872 and, since they played on Wimbledon Common, in 1890 became Wimbledon Ladies. Among the members was Miss Issette Pearson, who became largely responsible for the establishment of a governing authority, the Ladies Golf Union (LGU) in 1893.

It was not widely acclaimed, one letter informing the LGU that: 'Constitutionally and physically women are unfitted for golf. The first women's championship will be the last. They are bound to fall out and quarrel on the slightest, or no, provocation'. But within a few months the first British Women's Amateur championship was held over a nine-hole course at Lytham St. Annes, Lancashire, and won by Lady Margaret Scott, who repeated her success in 1894 and 1895 and then retired. The championship has remained a match-play tournament, as has the US Women's Amateur, other than in its inaugural year, 1895.

Oddly enough, there is not an equivalent body to the LGU in the United States, where women's championships, including the Open and Amateur, all come under the wing of the USGA which has a special women's committee to control their various events. An early three-time winner of the US Women's Amateur, Beatrix Hoyt, was only 16 when she triumphed for the first time in 1896. After completing her hat-trick in 1898 she, like Lady Margaret Scott, retired and it was not until 1971 that Laura Baugh relieved her of the distinction of being the youngest champion, at 16 years and two months. May Hezlet, who was 17 when she won the title in

Margaret and Harriot Curtis, donators of the Curtis Cup.

Laura Baugh, who won the United States amateur championship at the age of 16. She is now Laura Cole, having married the South African golfer, Bobby Cole.

1899 at Newcastle, Co Down, is the most junior British champion.

The other significant figures in women's golf were the American sisters, Margaret and Harriot Curtis, both in their time US champions as well as being early visitors to Britain. They played in the British championship at Cromer in 1905 and also took part in an unofficial international match. In 1930, the international experiment was tried again at Sunningdale and created such interest

that the sisters presented the Curtis Cup for regular competition between US and British women's teams. It was first contested at Wentworth, Surrey, in 1932 and, like the Walker Cup (1922) and the Ryder Cup (1927), which are the men's amateur and professional counterparts, has been held every two years ever since, other than in the war years.

America have been dominant in all three of these international confrontations and in the Curtis Cup it was

Right: An unprecedented moment as Lady Katherine Cairns, the non-playing captain, receives the Curtis Cup at Muirfield in 1952. It was Britain's first defeat of the Americans.

Below: 'Cecil' Leitch, who brought a new vigour to women's golf. Between 1914 and 1926 she won the British championship four times.

not until 1952 that Britain recorded the first of their two victories, at Muirfield, Scotland. The other came in the next home match, at Prince's, Sandwich, in 1956, and, with a tie two years later at Brae Burn, Massachusetts, this has been the only period that Britain could be said to have held the whip hand. Elizabeth Price, Frances Smith (née Stephens) and Jesse Valentine had the distinction of being on all three of those British teams.

A feature of women's golf has been the enormous change in style of dress. In the early years of the championships the women wore outfits down to their ankles and quite often hats which today would appear more suitable for Royal Ascot or afternoon tea to the accompaniment of a palm court orchestra. Sleeves were buttoned to the wrist and the LGU was consequently shaken to its foundations when, in the British championship of 1933 at Westward Ho!, an unknown but very striking figure, Gloria Minoprio, armed incidentally with only one club, appeared in trousers. How they would have reacted to some of today's scantily dressed young Amazons makes the mind boggle!

Even before Miss Minoprio, however, there had been signs of a new vigour in the women's game. Between 1914 and 1926 Miss 'Cecil' Leitch won the British championship four times, displaying a zeal and vigour that broke fresh barriers. This was a golden era for women's golf for her career coincided with that of Joyce Wethered, later Lady Heathcoat Amory, who not only matched those four victories but, by her elegance and simplicity of method, revealed a swing that in many quarters has been regarded as being without equal, even by a man.

Miss Wethered's four titles came between 1922 and 1929, an era that also produced, in 1927, the first European winner, the Frenchwoman Simone de la Chaune, later Madame René Lacoste. Her daughter, Catherine Lacoste, emulated her by taking the title at Royal Portrush in 1969, the year in which she also won the American Amateur. However, Catherine's greatest achievement was in becoming the first amateur to take the US Women's Open at Hot Springs, Virginia, in 1967, when she was also, at 22, the youngest champion.

Women's golf in America drew much inspiration from Alexa Sterling, champion three times in a row either side of the First World War, and Glenna Collett (later Mrs Edwin Vare) whose six championships between 1922 and 1935 remains a record. It beats by one the five titles that fell to JoAnne Gunderson (now the professional, JoAnne Carner) between 1957 and 1968.

While Dorothy Campbell, in 1909, and Pam Barton, in 1936, were British players who won both their own and the American championships in the same year, it is remarkable that it was not until 1947 that an American, Mildred (Babe) Zaharias, also took the British title, at Gullane, Scotland, though a number of her countrywomen have since emulated her.

Mrs Zaharias' brilliance at any sport she chose is legendary. When, therefore, she turned professional, it was both to her and Patty Berg, likewise a former amateur champion, that the instigators of a professional circuit turned. In 1946 a Women's Professional Golfers'

Joyce Wethered displays her fine balance at Burnham and Berrow in the 1923 British championship.

Association was formed (and with it the first Open championship) but quickly perished before being revived as the Ladies' Professional Golfers' Association (LPGA) in 1950.

It was Fred Corcoran, a former executive director of the men's professional tour, who foresaw the possibilities and, having made the initial soundings, issued the brief statement: 'There is a place for women's professional golf in this country'. As the LPGA's first tournament director, he raised 45,000 dollars for nine tournaments in 1950, most of the early prize money going to Miss Berg, the LPGA president, and Mrs Zaharias. Between them they won 19 of 23 tournaments in the first two years.

By 1970 the number of tournaments each season had risen to 21 and prize money to $750,000. However by the mid-1970s the LPGA was on the verge of bankruptcy before being hauled from the edge of the precipice by Ray Volpe, a marketing and advertising executive who, as Commissioner of the Association, raised prize money to $6.4 million in three years. It now stands at around $9 million a season and the women's professional circuit has become very much a part of the overall golfing scene in America.

The enormous improvement in the standard of play has been the major

contributing factor to this success and such as JoAnne Carner, Kathy Whitworth, Mickey Wright, Carol Mann and Nancy Lopez have all become household names. Already there are eight dollar millionairesses and it was inevitable that the British would explore similar avenues.

The British Women's Professional Golfers' Association was founded in 1979 and, after uncertain beginnings, is showing signs of gathering strength. It is now under the same roof as the men's PGA at Sutton Coldfield, near Birmingham, with prize money in 1985 exceeding £500,000 and likely to expand now that tournaments are beginning to mushroom in Europe as well. A Women's Open had already started in 1976, but in 1983 it had to be shelved for a year in the absence of a sponsor while only the intervention of the R & A salvaged it in 1985. Hopefully it will now survive.

Hollis Stacy, three times winner of the U.S. Women's Open, in 1977–78–84.

Left: Nancy Lopez, whose attractive personality was instrumental in making the LPGA tour a multi-million dollar circuit.

Overleaf: The scene on the final green of the British women's Open in 1984 at Woburn. Ayako Okamato, of Japan, is about to putt out for victory by 11 strokes.

The Ryder Cup and the Walker Cup

The British Ryder Cup team prepare to set sail for the inaugural match against the United States at Worcester, Mass, in 1927 – together with their mascot, who was merely seeing the team off. Left to right: George Duncan, Archie Compston, Ted Ray (capt), Fred Robson, Sam Ryder (donator of the cup), George Gadd, Charles Whitcombe, Arthur Havers, Abe Mitchell and the team manager, who was also secretary of the PGA, G.A. Philpott.

Though golf is, by its nature, very much an individual game, team golf imposes in many ways even greater demands in that the result of the whole match can, in the end, depend on just one player. This was never better illustrated than in the Ryder Cup match at Royal Birkdale in 1969 when, as twilight began to creep across the links, Great Britain were still locked with the United States at 15½–15½ with just one game to finish – and that all square as Tony Jacklin and Jack Nicklaus came to the 18th.

A fearful responsibility therefore lay on the shoulders of both players but what happened next captured perfectly the spirit and tradition of this biennial encounter between the professional golfers of the two countries. Both were on the green in two, but Jacklin putted up perhaps two feet (60cm) short of the hole, which under the circumstances made his next eminently missable. Nicklaus at once conceded the putt before knocking his own, rather shorter one into the hole for the half and a tied match. Nicklaus explained later that he would have hated to see Jacklin miss with so much resting on it.

It was certainly one of the most exciting finishes in Ryder Cup history, which goes back to 1927 when a St. Albans, Herts, seed merchant, Sam Ryder, donated a trophy that has been contested every two years since, other than during the Second World War. What inspired Ryder, it seems, was his delight when, in 1926, in an unofficial match at Wentworth, Britain hammered the Americans 13–1 to repeat an earlier victory at Gleneagles, Scotland in 1921.

The very sight of an actual trophy nevertheless stirred something in the breasts of the Americans. Since even exchanges in the first four Ryder Cup matches, US dominance has been almost embarrassingly one sided. The putt Syd

Robert Hudson, whose hospitality to the British team enabled the Ryder Cup to be resumed after the Second World War, presents the cup to Ben Hogan at Portland, Oregon, in 1947. On the left is Henry Cotton and on the right, next to Hogan, Ed Oliver.

Bernard Hunt hangs his head after missing the putt that would have tied the Ryder Cup at Wentworth in 1953. On the left is Dale Douglas, with whom Hunt halved his game.

Easterbrook holed at Southport and Ainsdale in 1933 to beat Densmore Shute on the final green in the last game to finish provided Britain with their last victory until 1957.

British funds were low after the war and the Ryder Cup was resumed at Portland, Oregon, in 1947 only because of the generosity of a local business man, Robert Hudson, who not only met the British team's travel costs but played host to them as well. The American team was less hospitable. They won by 11–1.

Nevertheless the match had been saved and at Ganton, Yorkshire, in 1949 Britain led after the foursomes before wilting under a counter-attack in the singles as Ben Hogan, still recuperating from a severe motor accident, spurred his troops to ever greater heights.

There was excitement, too, at Wentworth in 1953 as Britain turned the tables after losing the foursomes. With two games to finish they were ahead, but the responsibility was too much for two of the younger team members, Bernard

Right: Jubilation at Lindrick in 1957 as Max Faulkner congratulates Dai Rees (in jersey) after Britain had defeated the United States for the first time since 1933.

Below: Tony Jacklin (nearest camera) and Brian Huggett discuss the line to be taken from the tee during the 1971 Ryder Cup at St Louis. They halved their foursome with Lee Trevino and Mason Rudolph, but the USA won the match 16–11.

Jack Nicklaus takes advice from Arnold Palmer during the 1973 Ryder Cup match at Muirfield. They defeated Maurice Bembridge and Eddie Polland by six and five.

Hunt and Peter Alliss, and their mistakes at the 18th hole cost two points and turned victory into defeat.

But there was no mistake at Lindrick in 1957 when, under the inspiring leadership of Dai Rees, a determined little Welshman, Britain came back from a 3–1 deficit in the foursomes to take the singles 6–1 and the match by 7–4. The Americans have not lost since. At Palm Desert, California, in 1959 they easily recaptured the trophy and in an effort to maintain interest in the match, the format was slightly changed. Until then, play had been by four foursomes and eight singles, all over 36 holes. The longer distance is acknowledged as favouring the stronger players and in 1961 at Royal Lytham the play was cut to 18 holes. There were, however, now two sets of foursomes and singles to make up,

24 points now being at stake instead of only 12.

It made no difference, the USA winning comfortably. At Atlanta, Georgia, in 1963 fourball matches were introduced which added a third day to the series and put 32 points at stake. Again the United States cruised home, by 23–9, but the playing pattern was maintained, with Britain getting some encouragement with that tie in 1969. However there were now mutterings that 36 holes in a day for three days was too much for men in the prime of their physical careers (!) and in 1977, at Royal Lytham, there was a brief and unsuccessful experiment when play was cut to five foursomes, five fourballs and ten singles. While that may have been enough for the players, it was not enough for the spectators.

Opposite: An anxious
moment for Jack
Nicklaus, the American
captain, during the 1983
Ryder Cup. The
closeness of the match
is also reflected in the
expressions on the faces
of Tom Watson's wife,
Linda (seated on the
golf cart) and, on her
immediate right,
Barbara Nicklaus.

Again a change had therefore to be made in the format; back again to two series of foursomes, two of fourball and now 10 singles, making 28 points at stake. This has been the formula since 1979 other than one revolutionary step in a further attempt to shift the balance of power.

From the beginning the Ryder Cup had been between the United States and, to give the official title, 'Great Britain and Ireland'. However by this time the British circuit had been extended and attracted a number of Europeans, chief among them Severiano Ballesteros, of Spain, who won the Open in 1979. It was with him and others in mind that the 'British' selection was broadened to include players from the Continent of Europe.

Even that did not immediately make a noticeable difference, though in 1983, at the PGA National course in Florida, the Americans got the fright of their lives in a marvellously even tussle, never more than a point separating the two teams to the last moment as the States squeezed home by 14½–13½. Perhaps the greatest testimony to the Ryder Cup is that its tradition has been preserved and that places in the team are as eagerly sought as the biggest pay cheque.

Accident of birth

The highest honour an amateur can hope to attain is to play for his country in the Walker Cup match between the United States and Great Britain and Ireland. It was instituted in 1922, though in a sense by accident. The Walker Cup was intended to be an international competition, rather like today'sEisenhower trophy, which is now the world amateur team championship.

Such an idea began to be formulated in 1920 when a delegation from the USGA went to St. Andrews for a discussion with the R & A on the rules. The USGA's president, George Herbert Walker, was particularly taken with the idea of an international competition and on his return to the States offered to put up a cup.

In 1921 the USGA sent invitations to the various golfing nations inviting them to send a team to compete for the Walker Cup. They all declined, but the same year another American, George C. Fownes, who had twice raised teams to play against Canada, assembled another to challenge the British on the eve of the Amateur championship at Hoylake. A year later, in 1922, the R & A sent a side to America where they played the United

Right: The United
States capture the
Walker Cup for the
second time at Garden
City, New York, in
1924. From left to
right: William Fulowes
Morgan, president of
Garden City, Wyant
Vanderpeel, president of
the USGA, Cyril
Tolley, captain of the
British team, and
Robert Gardner, captain
of the Americans.

Right: Bobby Jones (right) and Rex Hartley, opposing players in the 1930 Walker Cup match which the USA won 10–2.

Below: Leonard Crawley, who put a dent in the Walker Cup when his approach to the 18th green at the Country Club, Brookline, in 1932, struck the trophy. Crawley beat George Voigt by one hole for Britain's solitary point.

States for the cup at George Walker's home club, the National links at Long Island, New York.

A return was held at St. Andrews in 1923 and a third at Garden City, NY, in 1924, all of which the Americans won. Since then the match has been a biennial affair, like the Ryder Cup and the Curtis Cup – and just as one-sided.

Yet US dominance has never detracted from the appeal of the Walker Cup, which in its early years involved some of the best golfers in the world, notable among them the American Bobby Jones. He made four appearances between 1924 and 1930 and was beaten only once, in his first foursome. He won all his singles, by four and three, 12 and 11, 13 and 12 and nine and eight, Cyril Tolley and Roger Wethered being among his victims. Tony Torrance, with three singles victories and a halved game in five appearances, had one of the best records among British players. Torrance won against Chic Evans in Chicago in 1928, when Britain were beaten 11–1, while at The Country Club, Brookline, in 1932 Leonard Crawley also recorded a solitary British victory but made an even more lasting mark when he dented the Walker Cup itself with an over-strong approach to the 18th green.

That the darkest hour is that before the dawn is certainly true of the Walker Cup. At Pine Valley, in 1936, Britain failed to win a single game but in 1938, with the match score 9–0 to the USA, the tide turned at last with victory under the captaincy of John Beck by 7½–4½. There could have been no better place for such a moment than St. Andrews itself, where all the British home matches had been held except that at Royal St. George's, Sandwich, in 1930.

The match returned after the Second World War when the Irishman, Joe Carr, made the first of ten successive appearances in 20 years between 1947 and 1967, a record without equal on either side. The United States nevertheless won again though the spirit of the match has never dimmed.

In 1953 at Kittansett, Massachusetts, for instance, an American player, James Jackson, discovered on the second fairway in the foursomes that he had more than the permitted 14 clubs in his bag. The penalty then was disqualification but Tony Duncan, the British captain, declared that he and his team had no wish

Left: Bill Campbell, who played in eight Walker Cup matches for the United States, found a bicycle the easiest means of transport in the British Amateur Championship at Muirfield in 1954. Campbell, later president of the USGA, reached the final but lost to a fellow American, Douglas Bachli.

Joe Carr, the redoubtable Irish international who made nine consecutive appearances in the Walker Cup beginning in 1947. He was also British Amateur champion on three occasions.

Right: Michael Bonallack, captain of the British team, lays his hand on the Walker Cup at St. Andrews. The outstanding British amateur golfer since the Second World War, Bonallack won the Amateur championship five times and is now secretary of the Royal and Ancient.

Below: Dr. David Marsh, who played the most celebrated shot of all in the 1971 Walker Cup. His three iron second to the 17th green on the last afternoon closed the door on Bill Hyndman III and secured the match for Great Britain and Ireland.

to win points that way. The penalty was modified to two holes and the American pair fought back to win. A British newspaper carried the rather splendid headline: 'Britannia waives the rules'.

A crushing 11–1 defeat at Seattle in 1961 nevertheless prompted a change in the playing conditions, which hitherto had always been over 36 holes, foursomes and singles. At Turnberry in 1963, two series of foursomes and two of singles, both over 18 holes, were introduced and this has been the pattern ever since.

Almost immediately there was a thrilling match at Baltimore, Maryland, in 1965, as Britain took a 10–4 lead with only eight singles to come. Suddenly however everything began to go dreadfully wrong and in the end it was only a putt of more than 30ft (9m) by Clive Clark that earned him a half on the 18th green and his country a tied match at 12–12.

That provided the necessary spur and in 1971, again at St. Andrews, Britain won for only the second time, under the captaincy of Michael Bonallack. The tables were turned late on the final afternoon as game after game suddenly swung, culminating in a three-iron shot Dr David Marsh hit to the 17th green to be sure of the vital point. It was a moment not to be forgotten.

Tournament golf

While the club professionals are always likely to be the backbone of the game, it is the tournament players who provide the shop window. There are three major circuits: the American Tour, the European Tour and the Japanese Tour, each lasting several months. Then there are the subsidiary circuits, like the Australian, South African and Asian, which run for shorter periods and depend, to some extent, on baiting the bigger fish from the bigger pools for 'guest appearances'.

The American PGA Tour is regarded as the First Division of the game. The prize money far exceeds that in Europe and Japan and the standard of play is also regarded as higher. As recently as 1975 the total tournament purse in the States was $7,895,450; by 1984 it had reached $21,251,382.

The forerunner to the present tour can be traced to the early 1920s, when a handful of tournaments were played during the winter months on the West

Left: All smiles beneath the Royal and Ancient clubhouse at St. Andrews as Joe Carr (left) congratulates his son, Roddy, who has just defeated Jim Simons on the last green. Enjoying the moment is Warren Humphreys.

Below: Fore! The shout echoes across the course at Sunningdale in 1948 as Sam King hooks his drive off the third tee, prompting spectators to take comic evasive action.

Above: Ken Schofield, executive director of the PGA European Tour. Behind him is Colin Snape, executive director of the PGA, and on the left are Jack Hargreaves, a past captain of the PGA and (seated) Lord Derby, president of the PGA.

Opposite: Tony Jacklin, whose victories in the British Open of 1969 and the US Open of 1970 gave British and European golf a valuable impetus.

Coast, and in Texas and Florida. Johnny Farrell, the 1928 US Open champion, recalls: 'Those tournaments gave the boys some activity in the off-season because most were busy at their clubs in the summer. The summer was when the golf associations would hold regional and national title events.'

With the emergence of such players as Walter Hagen, Gene Sarazen and the amateur, Bobby Jones, commercial companies and resorts recognized the publicity they could attract by holding tournaments. In 1934 Paul Runyan was leading money winner with $6,767 (in 1980, Tom Watson earned a record $530,808). Then came the likes of Sam Snead, Byron Nelson and Ben Hogan in the 1940s and 1950s.

But the real explosion began in the early 1960s when Arnold Palmer, the first of 48 dollar millionaires, was at his peak. Television enabled prize money to multiply many times over and tournament golf became big business with an increasing number of players employing

managers, of whom Mark McCormack became the most powerful. In 1968, the touring professionals took control of their own affairs with what was then called the Tournament Players' Division (TPD). Joe Dey, Executive Director of the USGA, took over as Commissioner, serving for five years before being succeeded by Deane Beman in 1974. Quite apart from the big increase in prize money since, Beman has masterminded the birth of the Seniors Tour for the over 50s, re-named the TPD as the PGA Tour and established new headquarters at Ponte Vedra Beach, Florida, with the first stadium golf course.

In many respects the PGA European Tour has followed that of the United States. Because of the climate, the season is necessarily a shorter one, beginning in April and lasting until November, when most of the later tournaments chase what remains of the sun into Spain.

At first, tournament golf was only a secondary responsibility of the Professional Golfers' Association, which

Above: Bernhard Langer, the West German who has twice been runner-up in the British Open, urges on a putt that declines to drop during the 1984 British Open at St. Andrews. The following April he had his reward, winning the Masters at Augusta.

Right: The manager has become a powerful influence in the game of golf. Here the most successful of them all, Mark McCormack, briefcase in hand, watches one of his most famous clients, Gary Player.

Deane Beman, executive director of the American PGA Tour since 1974. A former Walker Cup player, he won the US Amateur championship in 1960 and 1963 and the British Amateur in 1959.

was founded in 1901 mainly in the interests of the Club professionals. But the appointment of Commander Charles Roe in 1933 as secretary brought a greater awareness of the value of properly organized tournaments. Roe was succeeded by John Bywaters in the late 1950s and in the next 15 years or so there were many advances.

When the French, German, Swiss, Spanish and Scandinavian Open championships became part of the circuit in the 1970s, it was decided to set up a Tournament Players' Division (TPD).

John Jacobs, Britain's most respected teaching professional, was one of the moving forces behind the start of what has now become the PGA European Tour. Ken Schofield, who was appointed as secretary and is now Executive Director, can take much of the credit for the subsequent expansion. Prize money passed the £1 million mark in 1979 and in 1985 exceeded £4 million.

Tony Jacklin's victories in the British

Open in 1969 and the US Open in 1970 contributed much to the European boom, which was reflected in increased television coverage. Then, in the late 1970s came the young Spaniard, Severiano Ballesteros, and Bernhard Langer, of West Germany, the leading money winner in both 1981 and 1984, who made it inevitable that the British Ryder Cup team would become the European Ryder Cup team.

Certainly the European Tour is the most cosmopolitan in the world with players from many countries outside the continent competing regularly on the circuit. This is reciprocated to some extent when, in the winter months, the Europeans take off for South Africa and Australia. Visits are also made to Japan, which has made big strides in the past 20 years with prize money in excess of £5 million, and Asia, while such events as the Million Dollar Challenge at Sun City, Bophuthatswana, in Southern Africa, come as end-of-season rewards.

2 THE CHAMPIONSHIPS

While money may be the dominating factor in professional golf these days, winning a major championship still has a value far above monetary rewards. The British Open, the United States Open, the US Masters and the American PGA are together referred to as the Grand Slam, though no one has ever won them all in the same year.

The origins of the term spring from the performance of the American Bobby Jones, who in 1930 won both the Open and Amateur championships of Britain and the USA. It was an astounding performance, even by the greatest golfer of that time, amateurs then being a much stronger force than they are today.

Tournament play was still in its infancy and most professionals employed by a club were expected to give to it most of their time. There was consequently less incentive for the top-class amateur to turn professional.

It is most unlikely that any amateur could emulate Jones today. Professional standards have improved beyond all knowledge and as the world has shrunk beneath a cobweb of airline routes, so tournaments have sprung up somewhere almost every week of the year. It has bred a battle-hardened class of professional able to follow the sun in a manner beyond the means of anybody who plays the game simply for fun.

Bobby Jones in 1930, the year of his Grand Slam.

Nevertheless Jones had achieved something unique, and the only way of keeping the Grand Slam alive as some sort of mythical goal to the supreme golfer of his time was to change the qualifications. The two Open championships and the American PGA, an event under the jurisdiction of that country's professional parent body, were the leading tournaments in the years before the formation of the United States PGA Tour, which has different headquarters and now controls what could be described as the shop window of the game.

In 1934, Jones became involved in the building of a new course at Augusta National, in Georgia, and the launching of a tournament 'for a few of my friends'. He called it the Masters and it caught on almost at once. In 1935 Gene Sarazen, one of the great American golfers between the two World Wars, forced a tie by holing his second shot for an albatross (double eagle) at the par five 15th in the final round and then won the play-off the following day. The Masters immediately became front page news and although the tournament has, strictly speaking, remained invitational, the invitations are now by qualification and highly prized.

With its spring date in the calendar it was natural for the Masters to be regarded as launching a new season, it having both a ring to its name and also a most attractive setting amid the many flowering shrubs of a one-time nursery. The club was also farsighted enough in the 1950s to invite a number of British golf writers. So enchanted were they that the tournament quickly gained worldwide recognition which justified its inclusion in the modern Grand Slam.

The Americans also came to the rescue of the British Open, the oldest of all the major championships, which had slipped into decline compared to the 1920s and 1930s when Jones, Walter Hagen, Gene Sarazen and others made annual pilgrimages. But in 1960, the year of the Centenary Open, Arnold Palmer, who had become the great hero of American golf and at that time held both the Masters and the US Open, crossed the Atlantic to play at St. Andrews and finish second, a stroke behind Kel Nagle, of Australia. Palmer's visit restored in the eyes of other American golfers the importance of winning the Open if any of them were ever to regard themselves as the complete player.

In his wake came others, notable among them Jack Nicklaus, who was already in the process of taking Palmer's place as the best golfer in the world. At the same time the Royal and Ancient, the governing body of the Open, did their part nobly. By shrewd management and the expertise of a new secretary, Keith Mackenzie, prize money rapidly multiplied. In 1960 it stood at £7,000; in 1985 it was £530,000 and the Open, the most international of the four major championships, was restored to a premier place on the circuit.

Keith Mackenzie, who as secretary of the Royal and Ancient between 1967–83 played a leading part in the revival of the British Open.

The Open

Naturally enough it is all a distant cry from 1860 when the little fishing village of Prestwick, on the west coast of Scotland, staged the first Open. It was the brainchild of the club secretary, Major J. O. Fairlie. Strictly speaking it was not 'open' at all for there were only eight players and they were all professionals. However it did go some way towards establishing who was the successor to Allan Robertson, a St. Andrean who was regarded as almost unbeatable. He had died the previous year.

The big leather championship belt, presented by the Earl of Eglinton, was won on 17 October by Willie Park, of Musselburgh, with a total of 174 for the 36 holes, all of which were played in one day. Park had rounds of 58, 59 and 60, the course then comprising only 12 holes and measuring 3,799yd (3457m). The bogey (the equivalent of par today) was 48, or level fours. The *Badminton Library of Golf* records that the holes were for the most part 'out of sight when one took the iron in hand for the approach; for they lay in deep dells among the sandhills'.

Only one English club, Blackheath, was represented and though Park won by only two strokes from Tom Morris senior (his son 'Young Tom' being only nine years of age) there was a disparity of 58 strokes between the first and last places. However the championship was clearly a success since the amateurs, who had been barred, promptly made representations to the club and were admitted the following year. The championship has remained 'open' ever since.

Prestwick, a shrine to all golfers, has since been extended to 18 holes and, while something of a museum piece, has never lost its character and charm. In 1979 it was still regarded as good enough to stage the Scottish Amateur championship. It continued to host the Open until 1870, by which time the elder Morris had won four times and Park three. But by then Young Tom Morris had developed

The first green at Prestwick, site of the first Open championship in 1860. The wall runs alongside a railway line to the right of the fairway and has been the graveyard of many ambitions.

such a gift for the game that in 1868 he succeeded his father as champion. He was then only 17 but he not only set a championship record of 157 for the 36 holes but improved upon it in 1869 (154) and again in 1870 with 149, when he completed the first round 12 holes in 47, which was one under fours and quite remarkable considering his equipment and, of course, the gutty ball.

This hat-trick of victories nevertheless presented the club with a considerable problem, for the rules were that anyone who won the title three years in a row was entitled to keep the belt, which Young Tom did. As there was no trophy, 1871 became the only time, other than during the war years, when the Open has not been staged.

The Prestwick club then made approaches to the R & A and the Honourable Company of Edinburgh Golfers, whose home was then at Musselburgh, and between them the three clubs subscribed to the purchase of a silver claret jug, a permanent trophy

which the new champion retains for a year (or rather a replica of it, since the original remains under lock and key at St. Andrews) together with a gold medal as a permanent momento. Jamie Anderson (1877–79), Bob Ferguson (1880–82) and Peter Thomson (1954–56) all subsequently achieved Open hat-tricks.

Agreement was made that the three clubs would also take it in turns to stage the Open. On its revival in 1872 at Prestwick, Young Tom won yet again and his four wins in a row have never been equalled. Clearly it was a course that suited him. When the championship broke new ground at St. Andrews in 1873, he was joint third behind Tom Kidd and at Musselburgh the following year second to Mungo Park. Young Tom died, aged only 24, before the year was out.

A painting of Old Tom Morris, Open champion four times between 1861–67.

The move away from Prestwick provided variation of another sort, for St. Andrews was an 18-hole course, Musselburgh one of nine holes and Prestwick still one of 12 holes. Consequently the championship, while still of an overall length of 36 holes, now comprised two rounds of 18 holes at St. Andrews, three of 12 holes at Prestwick and four of nine holes at Musselburgh. The second Open at St. Andrews, in 1876, sparked dissension. Bob Martin and David Strath tied on 176 but there was a call for Strath's disqualification when he struck his approach to the 17th green with the golfers ahead still putting. This was against the rules at that time although one observer remarked that it was 'an abnormally long hit'. Strath took offence at the complaint and also at the committee's reluctance to come to a decision; he refused to play off and Martin was declared the winner.

It was Musselburgh that staged the first play-off, in 1883, Willie Fernie beating Bob Ferguson by a stroke over a second 36 holes. Two years later Bob Martin won for a second time at St. Andrews, a feat repeated since only by James Braid, J. H. Taylor and Jack Nicklaus.

It was not until 1890, at Prestwick, that the Scottish monopoly was brought to an end by John Ball, an amateur from the Royal Liverpool club at Hoylake, who became the first English champion, 12 years after, aged then 14, he had finished fifth on the same course. In 1892 a fellow club member of Ball's, Harold Hilton, gained the first of his two Open victories. He subsequently won the Amateur championship on four occasions and in 1911 became the only British golfer ever to have captured the US Amateur.

Hilton's win was at Muirfield (the Honourable Company by then having moved from Musselburgh) in the first Open to be played over 72 holes and extended to two days. Entry fees were also introduced and prize money tripled to more than £100. It was ironic that this new-found wealth should have coincided with only the second amateur winner.

The fields had also increased markedly in numbers and the decision was made to spread the wings of the championship. In 1894 it was taken to St. George's (not yet 'Royal') close to the little port of Sandwich, in Kent. Appropriately it was marked by the first victory by an English professional, J. H. Taylor, then of Winchester. Royal Liverpool was also included in championship venues, making five altogether, and it was there at Hoylake in 1897 that Hilton took his second title on his home course, much to the delight of the locals.

A wind of change was now blowing through the championship. Taylor's triumph at St. George's proved to be the dawn of a new era. It led to the emergence of what became known as The Great Triumvirate – Taylor, James Braid and Harry Vardon. Between them they dominated the 20 years leading up to the outbreak of the First World War when there were only five times when the Open was not won by one of them, Vardon taking six titles and the other two

The Open Championship belt Young Tom Morris won outright after three consecutive victories between 1867–69. It was then replaced by the present trophy.

JOHN HENRY TAYLOR
Open Champion
1894.1895.1900.1909.1913.*TIED* 1896.

JAMES BRAID
Open Champion
1901.1905.1906.1908.1910.

HARRY VARDON
Open Champion
1896.1898.1899.1903.1911.1914.

CLEMENT
FLOWER
1913

five each. Vardon's victory at Prestwick in 1898 was the first time 80 was beaten in every round, his scores being 79, 75, 77, 76.

In 1899 there was something of an uprising among the professionals arriving in Sandwich. They complained about the level of prize money and even talked of a strike. Trouble was averted principally because Vardon, who successfully defended his crown, Braid and Taylor were against such militancy. However the point had been made, and during the championship the first prize went up to £50.

Once Vardon had made the breakthrough of scoring 70s in each round, the next landmark was to get inside a total of 300 for the four rounds. It fell at length, in 1904, to Jack White, of Sunningdale, with an aggregate of 296 at the now Royal St. George's in a year of records. James Braid's third round of 69 was the first time anyone had broken 70, White's

Arnaud Massy, the Frenchman who became the first Open champion from overseas, in 1907.

concluding 36 holes of 141 (72, 69) stood for another 27 years and then J. H. Taylor rounded things off with another new low, a 68 in the fourth round. With the entry now 144, the championship was spread over three days.

The Triumvirate was still dominant, but at Hoylake in 1907 a Frenchman, Arnaud Massy, became the first from overseas to take the title. He had finished quite high in the 1902 championship on the same course and subsequently taken a club-making job in Scotland, where he married a local girl. Massy had therefore become familiar with British conditions. It was not until 1979 that another European, Severiano Ballesteros, of Spain, emulated him as Open champion.

Various permutations were being tried to control the expanding size of the fields as the title was swapped around between Vardon, Braid and Taylor, interrupted though they were by Ted Ray at Muirfield in 1912. At Prestwick in 1914 two qualifying rounds were tried with only 80 players advancing to the championship proper, but there was no consistency in the renovations, for the Open was now loosely controlled by a consortium of 26 clubs, the actual conduct of the championship being in the hands of the staging club each year.

A letter to the magazine *Country Life* just before the outbreak of the First World War from W. Herbert Fowler, a golf course architect who designed Walton Heath, Saunton and The Berkshire, had a profound influence. It read in part:

'It was in 1888 that the Royal and Ancient Golf Club gave to the world of golf the Rules of Golf. Since that time all clubs all over the world have played the game under those rules, and the Royal and Ancient Club has from time to time varied old rules and made new ones. The club, then, is the only authority which attempts to control the game, and it may be of interest to many golfers to consider how far that control goes; whether it is sufficient for present day needs, or whether the club should not be asked to go further than it does now and take charge not only of the rules of the game, but also of both championships [the Open and Amateur]. If the Royal and Ancient would appoint a golf committee of say 30 members, and hand over to them the whole control of the game there is little doubt that the clubs who are interested in the management of cham-

James Braid shows that fashions have changed more than golfing style in the last 60 years.

pionships would hand over their duties to such a body. There is one great difficulty in the way of this desirable end, and that is to find a means of satisfying the Royal and Ancient Club that there is any necessity to wake up and assert its authority and position'.

The R & A did wake up and thus it was that in 1919 their Championship committee came into being, controlling first the Open and Amateur championships and later the Boys' (1948), the Youths' (1963) and finally the Seniors' (1969). The Open itself was not resumed until 1920, when Royal Cinque Ports, Deal, became the venue for the first time, George Duncan the winner and prize money was increased to £225, with £100 for the winner.

The American invasion

A year later there came a significant turning point. For the first time the silver trophy found its way to America in the custody of Jock Hutchison, a St. Andrean who had emigrated to the States while still in his 'teens. He won after a play-off with an amateur, Roger Wethered, the brother of the famous woman golfer, Joyce. Wethered had to be persuaded to stay on for the extra day because he had previously arranged to play in a cricket match and did not want to let the side down! That it had been a tie at all may well have been due to a penalty stroke Wethered suffered in his third round when he inadvertently stood on his ball.

51

Above: A white line stops golfers from 'stealing' an inch or two in the 1923 Open at Troon. Walter Hagen in unsuccessful defence of his title.

Opposite top: A respectful audience watches Bobby Jones drive off at St. Andrews in 1927 when he successfully defended his title.

Of a sudden the floodgates were opened. At Royal St. George's in 1922 Walter Hagen won the first of his four titles in the space of eight years, launching an American domination that was to last until 1934, when Henry Cotton at last beat off the American invaders on the same course. Bobby Jones was champion three times during those years and Jim Barnes, Tommy Armour, Densmore Shute and Gene Sarazen once each. Barnes and Armour, like Hutchinson, had been born in Britain before emigrating to the States. Indeed Armour, who lost an eye during the First World War and in later life became one of the game's most respected teachers, had the novel distinction of playing for Britain in the Walker Cup and the USA in the Ryder Cup.

These in many ways were some of the most romantic years of the Open, for Hagen was a great favourite wherever he played. 'I don't want to be a millionaire, only to live like one', he would say, and was particularly noted for his colourful dress and dashing ways. In his first Open appearance, at Deal in 1920, he had finished a disappointingly long way behind the winner; but he promised to return, and was as good as his word.

In the three years beginning in 1922 Hagen was first, second and first again, only Arthur Havers getting the better of him when the championship was staged at Troon for the first time. It was there on the west coast of Scotland, incidentally, that a new American star, Gene Sarazen, made his debut, though he never got as far as the championship proper, failing to qualify in some wretched weather, of which he seemed to get the worst. Like Hagen, he said he would be back, though it was not until 1932 that he won.

Prestwick's long reign as an Open venue came to an end in 1925. It had played host on 24 occasions, which even St. Andrews has not yet surpassed. However Jim Barnes' victory provided final proof that it had become outdated. Huge crowds had hindered more than helped the Scottish-born Macdonald Smith, now resident in America, as he failed to make the most of a five-stroke lead going into the final round and, with an 82, finished fourth. The bottle-necks around the finishing holes proved quite unmanageable, and the respected British golf-writer Bernard Darwin was moved to comment: 'I gravely doubt whether a championship should be played there again'.

Royal Lytham's first Open in 1926 was notable for a first victory by the great Bobby Jones, who had already won the US Open once and the US Amateur twice. Having left the course for lunch after the third round (two rounds then being played on the final day) his identity was challenged by a gatekeeper when he returned and rather than make a fuss, Jones paid to get back in again. More celebrated was the five-iron shot he played from a little bunker to the left of the 17th fairway in the last round. It carried some 170yd (150m) over the intervening gorse to the green, the audacity of the shot prompting his opponent, Al Watrous, with whom Jones was tied at the time, to take three putts. A plaque marks the bunker from which Jones played the stroke and the club he used hangs in the Royal Lytham clubhouse.

Jones won more easily at St. Andrews the following year, setting a new championship record of 285. Thus began his fond association both with the Old course and the 'Auld Grey Toon' itself – an affection which had hardly seemed likely after his first Open there in 1921 when Jones' had torn up his card in frustration. But it was also at St.

Andrews in 1930 that he took the Amateur championship on the way to his Grand Slam and when, in 1958, he was given the freedom of the Burgh, Jones said in his address: 'I could take out of my life everything except my experience at St. Andrews and I'd still have a rich, full life'.

By 1928, when Hagen won for the second time at Royal St. George's and

Above: A confident Walter Hagen poses for the press at Sandwich in 1928. It proved to be the third of his four championships.

53

A youthful Henry Cotton watches his drive from the 10th tee at Muirfield in 1929. Walter Hagen is to his left.

the third time in all, the two qualifying rounds were being held on the Monday and Tuesday on two courses, one of them the championship course, the other, in this case, Prince's. The field then swapped over for the second 18 holes, the leading 100 or so advancing to the championship proper. This remained the pattern until as recently as 1963, when the better players became exempt from qualifying.

Still the Americans came and still they conquered; Hagen again in fierce winds at Muirfield in 1929, Jones the following year at Hoylake, Armour at Carnoustie and, in 1932, Sarazen at Prince's, just the other side of the fence from St. George's. Historically it was the victory by Jones in 1930 that meant the most. He had already won the British Amateur and within a matter of weeks he had added both the US Open and Amateur titles to complete the Grand Slam. Then he retired, aged 28.

Though Jones led throughout at Hoylake, his final round was not a complete triumph for he managed to take seven at the eighth without once being off the fairway. But he steadied im-

mediately, playing the last ten holes in one over fours for a round of 75 and victory by two strokes from Macdonald Smith and Leo Diegel. However the strain of championship golf was telling. He was frequently sick with apprehension and would sometimes lose nearly a stone (14lb/6.4kg) in weight during the week of a championship.

Similarly, Sarazen led from start to finish at Prince's in 1932, also beating the ever-consistent Macdonald Smith, who had the reputation of being the best golfer of his time never to win a major championship. Sarazen had been out of sorts in practice, but when he was reunited with his trusty old caddie, Daniels, who had also carried Hagen's bag, he became a new man. At first Sarazen had declined the Daniels' services, suspecting he might be too frail for 72 holes. Instead he proved an inspiration.

After the British victory in the 1933 Ryder Cup at Southport and Ainsdale, the Americans stayed on for the Open at St. Andrews and filled five of the first six places, Densmore Shute winning after a play-off with Craig Wood. This was of

Left: A ticker-tape reception for Bobby Jones, arriving in New York in 1930 after winning both the British Open and Amateur championships. Within a few weeks he had completed the Grand Slam.

Below: Henry Cotton on his way to Open championship victory at Royal St. George's in 1934 which ended 11 years of American domination.

some consolation to Shute. It was the defeat he had suffered at the hands of Syd Easterbrook at Southport that had decided the Ryder Cup.

Further British celebration came at Royal St. George's the following year as Henry Cotton brought to an end the long run of American domination of the Open. His opening rounds of 67 and 65 set a record still standing in 1984, but victory looked less than inevitable when Cotton was attacked by stomach cramps as he waited to start his last round. However, Cotton rallied after a dreadfully uncertain start – 40 to the turn and three more fives to follow – playing the last six holes in level fours for a 79 that still gave him plenty of margin.

The two Alfs, Perry and Padgham, were the next British champions before Cotton gained a second victory in 1937 as torrential rain flooded Carnoustie until the point where it was almost unplayable. In such conditions, Cotton's 72 and 71 through the worst of the weather on the final drenching day were in a class of their own and confirmed him as an outstanding champion. Gales marred the 1938 Open at Royal St. George's when only three players, Reg Whitcombe, the winner, Jimmy Adams and Cotton had totals of less than 300. Even the exhibition tent was destroyed. But storm clouds of another sort were gathering, though the holocaust of the Second World War did not break until after Dick Burton's win at St. Andrews in the summer of 1939.

Below: Alf Perry splashes clear of one of Muirfield's many deep bunkers in the 1935 Open.

Modern heroes

German prisoners of war helped to prepare St. Andrews when the championship was resumed in 1946. Prize money was also advanced to £1,000 and Sam Snead pocketed £150 of it with a comfortable victory by four strokes from Bobby Locke, a South African, and Johnny Bulla. However Snead played in the Open only once more, some years later. He was not enamoured with Britain, regarding it as 'camping out'. It may not have been too erratic a description; some of his opponents during that time had competed in their service uniforms.

Fred Daly, an Irishman, became champion at Hoylake in 1947, while Henry Cotton's third victory at Muirfield, in 1948, posed the question as to how many more he might have won but for the war. He beat Daly by five strokes and reserved his best round, a 66 on the second day, for King George VI, who was among the gallery. That was the end of Cotton's reign but he is still the only British player to have won three Opens since the days of Vardon, Braid and Taylor.

There then began the reigns of Bobby Locke and Peter Thomson, an Australian, who in the next ten years won the Open four times each (Thomson's fifth title coming later). The only others to interrupt this domination were Max Faulkner, at Royal Portrush in 1951, and Ben Hogan, at Carnoustie in 1953. Locke's first win at Royal St. George's in 1949 will always be remembered as the year of 'Harry Bradshaw's bottle'. The Irishman hit his drive to the fifth in the second round into a broken beer bottle, and, since it was difficult in those days to get an immediate ruling, he played the ball 'as it lay', glass and all. The hole cost him a seven and he eventually tied with Locke, who refused to go out for the play-off until the flag positions were moved, it being the practice then to keep them in the same places all week.

Faulkner was Britain's last Open champion until 1969, when Tony Jacklin won at Lytham. Royal Portrush also has the distinction of being the only Irish course given the honour of staging the Open. In many ways, however, it was Hogan's win at Carnoustie in 1953 that really captured the imagination of the British golfing public. Here was the supreme golfer of his time, triumphant already that year in both the Masters and the US Open, perhaps even more brilliant than he had been prior to a frightful motor accident a few years before, ruthlessly dismantling a great course with rounds ever lower than the last – 73, 71, 70, 68. It was a masterpiece of planning. Hogan had arrived a week early so that he could not only play and study the course in all weathers but familiarize himself with the smaller ball still in use in Britain.

Locke's first three victories had come in the space of four years (1949–50–52). He was an unusual player in that he hit everything, including his chips and putts, right to left. Thomson, who was just as immaculate if rather more orthodox, quickly caught him with three wins in a row, beginning at Birkdale in 1954 and including the first £1,000 win, at St. Andrews in 1955. There was bigger public interest, too, and in 1957 with the leaders going out last for the first time the concluding stages were shown live on television. It exposed an unusual incident involving Locke's last victory.

The championship had been switched at the last minute from Muirfield to St. Andrews because of a petrol shortage

Above: Max Faulkner at Royal Portrush in 1951 where he proved to be the last British winner of the Open championship until Tony Jacklin 18 years later.

Left: Balance, poise and a half smile of satisfaction as Ben Hogan tames Carnoustie in 1953.

Opposite bottom: Harry Bradshaw at Royal St. George's in 1949. He tied with Bobby Locke but lost the play-off.

Above: One of the more unnerving shots at St. Andrews. Peter Thomson chips over the Swilcan Burn to the first green in 1957.

Right: Bobby Locke at St. Andrews in 1957 where he became Open champion for the fourth time.

Gary Player hangs his head in despair after taking six at the last at Muirfield in 1959. His wife, Vivien, tells him not to despair and she proved to be correct. Player still won his first major championship by two strokes from Flory Van Donck, of Belgium, and Fred Bullock.

during the Suez crisis. Before Locke putted out for victory by three strokes from Thomson, he had marked his ball on the 18th green. However, he had forgotten that he had put his marker a few inches to one side and re-spotted the ball in the wrong place. It was noticed on television but the committee ruled, after lengthy deliberations, that it did not effect the result and both Locke's score and victory were allowed to stand.

The Thomson-Locke stranglehold was finally broken in 1959 by another South African, Gary Player, who was to make a great impact on the game. The last two rounds were still being played in one day and over these 36 holes Player came from eight strokes behind to win, even though he took six at Muirfield's last hole. Prize money had now gone up to £5,000 and the Open was about to 'take off'.

It was Arnold Palmer who lit the fuse, lured by the Centenary Open at St. Andrews in 1960. Already Masters and US Open champion that year, he went very close to a third major championship, finishing just a stroke behind the Australian, Kel Nagle. But Palmer was back again to win at Birkdale the following year and again at Troon in 1962. He conquered a gale at Birkdale and then overcame a fast-running course at Troon to finish six ahead of Nagle and no less than 13 strokes clear of those in third place, setting an aggregate record of 276. It was at Troon, incidentally, that Jack Nicklaus made his first appearance, already US Open champion in his rookie year as a professional. His impact was minimal and he only just qualified for the last two rounds. But it was not long before the championship was reverberating to the thunder of his golf.

In 1963 Nicklaus was third to the New Zealander Bob Charles, and in 1964 second to Tony Lema. Charles, who won a play-off against American Phil Rodgers, at Royal Lytham, is the only left-hander to have won any of the four major championships. Lema might well have become one of the great players. He had an elegance and style that was never more obvious than at St. Andrews when, despite only one full practice round, he still won by five strokes. Tragically, he was killed in a flying accident two years later.

Four of Thomson's victories had come before the American invasion, but he abundantly proved his class in 1965 at Royal Birkdale as he eclipsed a field that included Palmer, Lema and Nicklaus. Although on this occasion Nicklaus finished well back, his culminating moment was not far away. Nicklaus had first played in Britain in the 1959 Walker Cup match at Muirfield and it was there in 1966 that he gained the first of his three championships, mastering a course that was in places waist deep in rough. His last round of 70 just held off the challenges of the Welshman David

Thomas and another American, Doug Sanders, who was to be thwarted again in much more trying circumstances a year or two later. For the first time the format ran over four days, one round each day.

By contrast to Lema, and later Tom Watson, both of whom won the Open at their first attempts, it took Roberto de Vicenzo, of Argentina, 19 years before at last he took the title at Hoylake in 1967. He had been second and third a number of times but his modesty and gentle humour always made him a great favourite. It was the last time Hoylake staged the Open, unable now to cope with an expanding tented village and crowds approaching 50,000.

Player's second victory in 1968 was a high-scoring one as Carnoustie measured a massive 7,252yd (6,600m) and there was great British jubilation the following year when Tony Jacklin brought to an end 18 years without a home winner as he beat Bob Charles by two strokes at Royal Lytham. When Jacklin then went out in 29 in the first round the following year at St. Andrews, a successful defence of the title looked a distinct possibility. But a thunderstorm

In vile weather Arnold Palmer played some of the finest golf of his career in winning his first Open at Royal Birkdale in 1961.

Golf may be an all-weather game but there are days when play becomes impossible. Here Henry Cotton (right) and Ralph Morfitt make their way back to the clubhouse after play had been suspended at Royal Birkdale in 1961.

Below: The famous Arnold Palmer 'twirl' as he destroys the field at Troon in 1962.

which flooded the course interrupted him; play was suspended until the following day and the magic was gone.

Instead it was Nicklaus who won after a play-off (the first to be staged over only 18 holes) against Doug Sanders. To be champion at St. Andrews, the home of the game, meant a great deal to Nicklaus. On sinking his winning putt he threw his club high in the air, there being some danger of it descending on Sanders' head. But the sympathy was very much with Sanders for he had come tantalizingly close to winning before the play-off. He had missed a putt of three feet (90cm) for the title on the 72nd green with Nicklaus looking on helplessly.

The 100th Open, coming after the Centenary Open, was won by Lee Trevino in 1971 at Royal Birkdale after a very stout chase from a little known Taiwanese, Liang Huan Lu, who quickly became known as 'Mr. Lu' as he politely raised his little pork-pie hat every time the crowds applauded his shots. Within a matter of weeks Trevino had taken the US, Canadian and British Opens and a year later he was back to win again at Muirfield. Trevino nevertheless had most of the luck on this occasion since he holed two chips and a bunker shot in the last 21 holes. The chip he sank from behind the 17th green in the last round to save par completely shattered

Jack Nicklaus in his 'heavier' days of the early 1960s.

Bob Charles, of New Zealand, the only left-hander to have won any of the world's four major championships, closes in on victory in his Open play-off against Phil Rogers at Royal Lytham in 1963.

The 13th green at Muirfield in 1966 with Tony Lema chipping.

Roberto de Vicenzo,
one of the most popular
winners of the Open.

Jacklin, who fell a stroke behind when it seemed certain he would lead.

Tom Weiskopf overcame some thoroughly miserable weather at Troon in 1973 to equal Palmer's record of 276, while a year later Player triumphed for the third time at Royal Lytham, where the larger ball was made compulsory. He led from first to last, though he had a long and anxious search for his ball on the 17th hole in the last round before having to chip left-handed to the 18th green when his approach came to rest against the clubhouse.

There was a closer finish at Carnoustie in 1975, Tom Watson beating the Australian, Jack Newton, after they had tied over the 72 holes, to begin a period of extraordinary domination with no less than five victories in ten years – at Turnberry in 1977, Muirfield in 1980, Royal Birkdale in 1982 and Royal Troon in 1983. But these were also the emerging years of Severiano Ballesteros, the Spaniard who first made his presence felt at Birkdale in 1976. When, as a raw but exciting 19-year-old, he led for three rounds before losing to the American Johnny Miller's greater experience over the last 18 holes.

Yet of all the recent Opens it is that at Turnberry in 1977 that stands out as brightly as the gleaming white light-house that guards the far end of the course. It was here that Watson and Nicklaus were at one another's throats from first to last, nothing separating them for three days as they each went 68,

Overleaf: Neil Coles drives through the rain at St. Andrews in 1970.

Below: A great moment for British golf as Tony Jacklin receives the Open championship trophy from Lord Derby at Royal Lytham in 1969.

65

Above: When Jack Nicklaus came to the 18th in his play-off with Doug Sanders at St. Andrews in 1970, he peeled off his yellow pullover before driving through the green 354yd (322m) away. Here, his sweater on again, he chips back, and a minute or so later holed the putt that made him champion.

Right: Lee Trevino shows his delight as he holes an important putt at Royal Birkdale, where he won the championship in 1971.

Liang Huan Lu, better known as 'Mr Lu', who chased Trevino all the way at Royal Birkdale.

70, 65. Nor was there anything between them until the 17th hole in the final round when Watson had a birdie and Nicklaus did not. Both had birdies at the last and Watson was home by a stroke with another 65 to Nicklaus' 66. Hubert Green, third 11 strokes behind, said that he had won 'the other tournament' and Watson's total of 268 broke the record by eight strokes.

Watson also shared the lead after three rounds at St. Andrews in 1978, but this time he faded and Nicklaus came through at the last gasp to overtake four players, among them the New Zealander, Simon Owen, who had led with three holes to play. It was Nicklaus' third victory, and his second at St. Andrews. When he tied second at Royal Lytham in 1979 he had the astonishing record of having finished in the top three 13 times in 18 years.

But Lytham '79 was the year of Ballesteros as he overtook and then

Opposite left: The young and still raw Severiano Ballesteros at Royal Birkdale in 1976.

Left: At the height of their memorable battle for the 1977 Open championship at Turnberry, Jack Nicklaus (left) and Tom Watson had to take shelter while a thunderstorm passed.

Opposite right: 'I've got it'. Tom Watson is unable to restrain himself as he holes for a birdie on the last green at Carnoustie in 1975 to earn a play-off with Jack Newton, of Australia.

Below: One of the wetter Opens, at Troon in 1973: Tom Weiskopf (centre) takes a ruling from Johnnie Salvesen, of the R & A championship committee, while Bob Charles (left) looks on.

demoralized Hale Irwin in the final round, hitting his then inevitable quota of wild shots but recovering brilliantly time and time again. He was the first Continental winner since Arnaud Massy in 1907 and the attendance touched a new record of 134,571 with prize money, now going up by leaps and bounds, £155,000.

Watson's victory at Muirfield in 1980, which saw the first Sunday finish other than in a play-off, was an unexceptional one, though scoring was low. Watson had a third round of 64 and Isao Aoki, of Japan, a 63, equalling the Open record by Mark Hayes at Turnberry in 1977. Bill Rogers' success when the championship returned to Royal St. George's after an interval of 32 years in 1981 also lacked sparkle. There was more excitement at Royal Troon in 1982 and at Royal Birkdale in 1983.

Each time Watson was the winner, though it hardly looked that way at Troon when Nick Price, a young South African, led by three strokes with only six holes to play. However Troon has a formidable finish, particularly when the wind is against; Price made mistakes and Watson did not. This was equally true of Watson at Royal Birkdale in 1983 when, needing a four at the last to beat Hale Irwin and Andy Bean, he hit two of the most perfect strokes, the second with a two iron, to the middle of the green. Irwin was consequently to rue an extraordinary lapse in the third round when he went to tap in a one inch (2.5cm) putt and, in his haste, missed the ball altogether.

St. Andrews therefore gave Watson the chance of a hat-trick as well as a sixth victory to match Vardon's record. But it was not to be, for Ballesteros, with whom

Above: Heads together as Gary Player (left) and Jack Nicklaus mark their putts at Royal St. George's in 1981.

Opposite: Half an hour earlier Simon Owen (left), of New Zealand, almost had the 1978 Open in his grasp, but now it is the time to congratulate the champion, Jack Nicklaus.

Overleaf: One of sport's crowning moments. The crowd rise to Severiano Ballesteros as he holes the winning putt at Royal Lytham in 1979.

Watson was locked for the whole of the final afternoon, played the 17th and 18th in 4, 3 while Watson took 5, 4 and that was the difference between them. So great were the crowds, 187,753, that prize money was increased by 10 per cent in mid-championship to £451,000, the half million being broken in 1985.

The US Open

The United States Open has a much more limited horizon than its British counterpart because it now attracts an entry of some 5,000. Reducing that number to a final field of 150 is a lengthy and hazardous business with only a limited number of places available at the various venues. Foreign players are therefore reluctant to commit themselves to a long stay in the States when their chances of 'lasting the distance' are accordingly that much more remote. For that reason the US Open is still predominately an all-American event.

The other main difference between the two is that while the British Open has now been played on 14 different courses, the USGA has taken their Open to 47 in an understandable policy to spread their gospel far and wide, mostly to courses near the major cities.

In the beginning the US Open was something of an afterthought to the US Amateur, to which it is junior by two years. The first was played the day after the Amateur in 1895, at Newport, Rhode Island, a nine-hole course on which Horace Rawlins, the home professional, had rounds of 45, 46, 41, 41. Rawlins was just one of a number of British professionals who had emigrated to the States when the game there was still in its infancy and consequently they reigned supreme. Even so it was not until 1900, by which time the championship had already been extended to 72 holes, that the trophy was taken out of the country, by Harry Vardon, who beat J. H. Taylor by two strokes at Chicago. It was the culmination of a year-long tour they made of the States, Vardon hardly losing a match and making the American public much more golf conscious.

Willie Anderson, Scottish-born but a young man who really learned to play in America, won four times in five years between 1901 and 1905 and his hat-trick, beginning in 1903, has never been equalled although his four victories have been subsequently matched by Bobby Jones, Ben Hogan and Jack Nicklaus.

Above: A champion's welcome as Tom Watson breaks through the crowd and advances on the 18th green at Royal Birkdale in 1983.

Opposite: The moment of truth for Nick Price, of South Africa, as his putt to tie at Royal Troon in 1982 fails to drop, leaving Tom Watson champion. With six holes to play, Price had been three strokes clear.

Left: A sixth Open begins to slip from Tom Watson's grasp as he chips from beside the 17th green in the last round at St. Andrews in 1984.

Unrestrained delight by Severiano Ballesteros as he holes his putt for a birdie to win the Open for a second time, at St. Andrews in 1984.

Alex Smith, with a score of 295 at Onwentsia, Illinois, was in 1906 the first man to score inside 300 for the four rounds, while in 1909 at Englewood, New Jersey, David Hunter became the first to break 70, having a 68 in the first round. George Sargent was nonetheless the winner, his total of 290 being the lowest so far.

In 1910 at Philadelphia came the first three-way tie involving the brothers Alex and Macdonald Smith and Johnny McDermott. Alex Smith won for a second time, but McDermott's hour was not long delayed. The following year at Chicago he became the first American-born champion, curiously after another three-way tie, this time with Mike Brady and George Simpson. And just to prove that it was no fluke, McDermott triumphed again at Buffalo, New York, in 1912, this time without the need of a play-off.

But the turning point for American golf has always been regarded as the 1913 championship at The Country Club, Brookline, Mass. The reason for this was

that Harry Vardon, who had by then won five British Opens, and Ted Ray, who had won one, the previous year, had crossed the Atlantic and tied with an unknown American amateur, Francis Ouimet. Vardon wrote subsequently that he and Ray had eyes only for one another in the play-off. Ouimet was, after all, only 20 and a member of the Woodland, Massachusetts, club having earlier been a caddie at The Country Club. Yet Ouimet provided the sort of shock that would today attend a young English amateur defeating Watson and Nicklaus. Ouimet had a 72 to Vardon's 77 and Ray's 78 and at once the American public was seized by a passion for the game.

The floodgates were opened in 1914, when the flamboyant Walter Hagen, who enjoyed a life-style that was to improve the lot of every professional the world over, won at Midlothian, Illinois, while two more amateurs, Jerome Travers and Charles Evans, not only emulated Ouimet but, in the case of Evans, set a new championship record of 286 at

Above left: Only a handful of British professionals have made the journey to America and returned with the US Open Championship. Harry Vardon was the first, in 1900 at Chicago.

Above: Ted Ray, the last British winner of the US Open until Tony Jacklin in 1970. Ray won 50 years earlier at Inverness, Ohio.

Francis Ouimet, whose
US Open victory in
1913 changed the course
of American golfing
history.

Minikahda, Minnesota. There was no
Open during the war years of 1917 and
1918 but Hagen triumphed a second
time at Brae Burn, Massachusetts, the
following year. Britain's by now suspect
role as the masters of golf flowered again
briefly at Inverness, Ohio, in 1920, when
Ted Ray, who had been involved in that
play-off against Francis Ouimet seven
years earlier, again made the voyage
across the Atlantic with Vardon, and was
this time the winner, Vardon being
among a group of four sharing second
place a stroke behind. Ray was the last
Briton to hold the US Open until Tony
Jacklin emulated him 50 years later.

However this 1920 championship was
a landmark for other reasons: it marked
the first appearance of the 18-year-old
amateur, Bobby Jones, who tied eighth;
it was also the first time that the host club
allowed the professionals full facilities,
which was something for which Hagen
had been agitating for many years.
Typically for him, Hagen promptly
organized a collection among his fellow
competitors and with the proceeds
presented Inverness with a grandfather
clock. It stands to this day in the main
lobby, bearing the inscription:
God measures men by what they are
Not what they in wealth possess.
This vibrant message chimes afar
The voice of Inverness.

Warren G. Harding, then President of
the United States, presented the trophy
to Jim Barnes at Columbia, Maryland, in
1921 while 12 months later at Skokie,
Illinois, a beaming, olive-skinned young
man of Italian extraction, Gene Sarazen,
caused an upset by winning at the age of
20. A last round of 68, which included a
birdie at the 18th, was the beginning of
an illustrious and lasting career.

It was at Inwood, New York, in 1923,
that the Bobby Jones era really began
with the first of four Opens in the space
of eight years, others following at Scioto,
Ohio, in 1926, Winged Foot, New York,
in 1929 and Interlachen, Minnesota, in
1930, the year of his Grand Slam. In the
intervening years Jones lost play-offs to
Willie Macfarlane at Worcester, Massachusetts, in 1925, and Johnny Farrell
at Olympia Fields, Illinois, in 1928 (both
over 36 holes), and was second to Cyril
Walker at Oakland Hills, Michigan, in
1924. It is a record of consistency
without equal, given further emphasis by
his five US Amateur championships
between 1924 and 1930.

Jones was simply a colossus, writing
chapter after chapter of American
golfing history and understandably
becoming the 'darling' of the galleries on
both sides of the Atlantic, especially so
when, in 1926, he became the first man to
take both the British and US Opens in
the same year. The whole world of golf
was then urging him towards the Grand
Slam and it finally arrived in 1930 after
victories first in the British Amateur at

St. Andrews and then in the Open at Hoylake.

At Interlachen Jones led the US Open by five strokes after three rounds but he still had to make three birdies in the last five holes, including a 40ft (12m) putt on the last green to beat Macdonald Smith. A few weeks later Jones moved serenely to his last US Amateur at Merion, Pennsylvania, for the completion of what he liked to call the 'Impregnable Quadrilateral' and, still only 28, retired. Golf, it is safe to say, will never see his like again.

By now gate money was being charged and prize money was in excess of $2,000. But though play-offs had been extended, temporarily as it happened, to 36 holes, it was still not enough to separate Billy Burke and George von Elm at Inverness in 1931. Level after 72 holes, they were still level after another 36 before Burke squeezed home by a stroke over the next 36. Their 144-hole battle remains unique.

A few weeks after he had won the 1932 British Open at Prince's, Gene Sarazen returned to the States to record his second US Open victory at Flushing Meadow, New York, and become the second man, after Jones, to take the two Opens in the same year. He had been seven strokes behind as he came to the ninth hole in the third round at Flushing but then played the last 28 holes in 100 strokes – a two at the ninth followed by 32 home and then a final round of 66. It was one of the most sustained spells of brilliance the game had ever seen.

Sarazen's total of 286 tied Chic Evans' record of 16 years earlier, while his 66 was an all-time low.

This was also the first US Open in which the 1.68in (4.3cm) ball was used. It differed slightly from the so-called 'balloon ball' which had been tried experimentally and optionally for a couple of years and was of the same diameter but lighter in that it weighed 1.55oz (43.9gm). The new ball, which was not used in the British Open until 1974 and did not really win world-wide approval until the early 1980s, replaced the smaller 1.62in (4.2cm) ball, though both weigh 1.62oz (46gm).

The Hogan era

The last amateur to take the US Open was Johnny Goodman in 1933, though he made heavy weather of a commanding lead at North Shore, Illinois, winning by a stroke. This was the same margin as Olin Dutra had at Merion, Pennsylvania, a year later. In this case however Dutra came from eight strokes behind with 36 holes to play as he edged past Sarazen. Prize money had now increased to $5,000 and, almost as if in response, the record tumbled twice in the next two years. Tony Manero lowered it by four strokes with a total of 282 at Baltusrol, New Jersey, in 1936 and then Ralph Guldahl brought it down by another one at Oakland Hills, Michigan, before retaining the trophy at Cherry Hills, Colorado, in 1938.

Somehow the title was always to elude

In 11 years, beginning in 1920, Bobby Jones won the US Open four times and was runner-up on another four occasions.

Lawson Little, who had won both the British and American Amateur championships twice, was also good enough to take the US Open at Canterbury, Ohio, in 1940.

Sam Snead. He was second to Guldahl in 1937 and he ought to have won at Philadelphia in 1939 but took eight at the last hole when, it ultimately transpired, a par five would have done. Snead did not even make the three-man play-off, which provided Byron Nelson with his solitary success after 36 holes.

Unlike the British Open, which was discontinued between 1940 and 1945, the US Open continued through 1940 and 1941. Lawson Little, a former amateur champion, won at Canterbury, Ohio, and Craig Wood at Colonial, Texas, respectively. Little had to go

another 18 holes after tieing with Sarazen, who came tantalizingly close to his third title 18 years after his first. Six players were also disqualified after 'playing away' before their official starting times in a bid to beat an impending thunderstorm. One of them, Ed Oliver, returned a score of 287, which would have tied with Little and Sarazen had it counted.

Prize money in the first post-war US Open at Canterbury, Ohio, in 1946, rose to $8,000, of which $1,500 went to the winner, Lloyd Mangrum. Having taken part in the Normandy landings, been

wounded and decorated with the Purple Heart, he was a hero in two respects. It nevertheless took him 108 holes to win for both Byron Nelson and Vic Ghezzi, with whom he had tied, were still level after another 18 holes, Mangrum beating them both by a stroke over the next 18. Earlier Nelson had been the victim of a penalty stroke when his caddie accidentally kicked his ball.

Snead again went close at St. Louis, Missouri, in 1947, losing a play-off to Lew Worsham when he missed a putt of less than a yard (0.9m) on the last green, while it was at Riviera, California, in 1948, that Ben Hogan's long wait came to an end. He had been favourite before and he won in the sort of style expected of him, shattering Ralph Guldahl's record by five strokes with a 72-hole aggregate of 276. But Hogan was unable to defend at Medinah, Illinois, for early in 1949 he was severely injured in a motor accident. There were fears that he might never play again. In his absence Dr Cary Middlecoff, who had qualified as a dentist but concentrated instead on becoming a most proficient tournament player, won by a stroke, Snead again being second.

The US Open was the one major championship constantly to elude Sam Snead.

Right: Ben Hogan, the only man who has won the US Open, Masters and British Open in the same year – 1953.

Far right: Ed Furgol, who made light of a childhood accident which left him with a withered left arm. His finest moment came when he won the US Open at Baltusrol in 1954.

Below: Kel Nagle, Australian winner of the 1960 British Open, also tied for the 1965 American Open at Bellerive but lost the play-off to Gary Player.

Hogan emerged from his accident an even more formidable player, winning three US Opens, two Masters and the British Open. His triumph at Merion in 1950 really caught the imagination. His once mangled legs were still so painful that it was difficult for him even to walk and he would leave his caddie to retrieve the ball from the hole. The last thing he wanted therefore was a play-off. But a play-off he got. Lloyd Mangrum and George Fazio tied his total of 287 but Hogan then destroyed them both with a 69.

It was at about this time that the USGA became a little paranoic about properly testing their champions; fairways became narrower, rough deeper and at Oakland Hills in 1951 the course was so severe that the professionals were on the verge of revolt. But Hogan vowed 'to bring this monster to its knees' and did so with one of his most brilliant final rounds, a 67 to defeat Clayton Heafner, who was the only other player to record a round of less than 70, by two strokes.

Some players reach the top quicker than others. Julius Boros was one. His victory at Northwood, Texas, in 1952, came only three years after he had turned professional. Hogan was third, but 12 months later at Oakmont the great man became champion for a record-equalling fourth time – and so comprehensively that he had six strokes to spare over Sam

Snead, second yet again. This was also the year in which Hogan went closest to completing the modern version of the Grand Slam. He had already taken the Masters and, after Oakmont, crossed the Atlantic to win the British Open at Carnoustie. Alas, he was denied the chance of going for the PGA, in which he had already triumphed twice, for there was insufficient time for him to get home again. No other professional has won three major championships in the same season.

Ed Furgol also overcame severe physical handicap to win at Baltusrol, New Jersey, in 1954. A playground accident in childhood had left Furgol with a badly broken left arm that did not receive skilled medical attention. The result was that it was both withered and permanently bent at some 70 degrees. Only great determination overcame his disability and Baltusrol was undoubtedly his finest hour. It was a notable championship in other ways: the entry 1,928, record crowds of nearly 40,000, all fairways roped from tee to green, national television coverage and prize money of $23,800 dollars.

Tieing with Furgol going into that last round was Hogan, whose expected fifth victory failed to materialize. But it was nothing like the shock that followed at Olympic, San Francisco, in 1955. Hogan appeared to be the certain winner until Jack Fleck, a municipal course professional playing the tour for the first time, caught him on 287 with two birdies in the last four holes. Even so, Fleck was given little chance in the play-off. However he won with a 69, Hogan burying his last flickering hopes by hooking his drive at the 18th into deep rough and taking three more to get back to the fairway. So far as Hogan was concerned it was the end of an era; but another was about to begin.

There was nothing exceptional about Arnold Palmer's Masters' victory in 1958; but there was about his second win at Augusta in 1960 when, needing two birdies to beat Ken Venturi, he duly got them. If this was thrilling stuff, it was nothing to Palmer's finish a month or two later in the Open at Cherry Hills. Trailing by seven strokes going into the last round, Palmer had six birdies in the first seven holes, went out in 30 and, with a closing 66, won by two strokes. Thus was born the famous 'Arnold Palmer charge'.

He was also that year within a stroke of Kel Nagle in the British Open at St. Andrews. Suddenly Palmer was 'all the rage': the golf glove stuck carelessly half in and half out of the hip pocket, the casually thrown cigarette before he putted, the whiplash finish to his follow-through. Yet the US Open was a championship Palmer won only once. Second to him at Cherry Hills was a promising young amateur, Jack Nicklaus.

In 1961 Nicklaus was fourth behind Gene Littler at Oakland Hills while in 1962, his first year as a professional, he became champion, having the effrontery to beat Palmer in a play-off at Oakmont. On greens which Sam Snead once compared to trying to stop a ball half-way down a marble staircase, Nicklaus took three putts only once in 90 holes while Palmer three-putted 10 times. Prize money had now reached $60,000 and the entry 2,453.

Few players have had the gift for swinging the club with such effortless grace as Gene Littler, US Open champion in 1961.

Right: It was this sort of bunker shot that enabled Billy Casper to overtake Arnold Palmer in the 1966 US Open at Olympic, California.

Below: Jack Nicklaus in 1967, when he won the championship at Baltusrol.

Above: Gary Player, of South Africa, in his younger days. He first won the US Open at Bellerive, Missouri, in 1965.

Record days

For Nicklaus, who had already won the US Amateur Championship in 1959 and 1961, it was the first of his 17 majors as a professional in the space of 19 years, well in excess of Jones' 13. Perversely Nicklaus then missed the 36-hole qualifying cut at the Country Club, Brookline, in 1963, Julius Boros, at 43, becoming the oldest winner since Ted Ray in 1920. Ray was the elder by less than a month. There were also stirring deeds at Congressional, Washington, the following year for Ken Venturi was in a state of collapse in oppressive heat and humidity as he won by four strokes. It was the last time 36 holes were played in a day, Venturi being examined by a doctor at lunch after a third round of 66 before being allowed to continue. Almost by instinct he got round again, in 70.

Another milestone was reached at Bellerive, Missouri, in 1965 when Gary Player, of South Africa, became the first overseas player to win since Ray, beating another non-American, Kel Nagle, of Australia in a play-off. Player gave all but

$1,000 of his $26,000 dollar first prize back to the USGA, to be distributed for cancer relief and the development of junior golf.

Palmer was still a considerable force but, so far as major titles were concerned, the point of no return came in 1966 at Olympic, San Francisco. He failed to defend a seven-stroke lead with nine holes to play and lost in a play-off to Billy Casper after leading by two strokes at the turn. The next year Nicklaus struck again, breaking Hogan's record by a stroke with total of 275 at Baltusrol, leaving Palmer second, four strokes behind. At once the record was equalled, but from an unlikely quarter, as the then little-known Lee Trevino became in 1968 the first man to score in the 60s in every round (69, 68, 69, 69) at Oak Hill.

By 1969 prize money had passed the $200,000 mark and Orville Moody, who had spent 14 years in the army, won at Champions, Texas, in only his second full season on the tour. Then at Hazeltine, Minnesota, Tony Jacklin became the first British champion in 50 years as he destroyed the field on a brutally long, windswept and severe course that was heavily criticized by a number of American players, among them Dave Hill, the runner-up, who was heavily fined for his remarks. Jacklin was the only player under par and won by seven strokes, a margin exceeded only by Willie Smith in 1899 and Jim Barnes in 1921. He was also the reigning British Open champion and his victories had a profound effect on British golf.

The ebullient Trevino struck again at Merion in 1971 (a year in which he was also to win the Canadian and British Opens in a matter of weeks) defeating Nicklaus in a play-off. However Nicklaus triumphed for a third time 12 months later in the first Open at Pebble Beach, California, where he had won the Amateur championship in 1961.

Another record was broken in 1973 at Oakmont where Johnny Miller had the lowest individual round, a 63 in the last to come from 'nowhere'. It contrasted sharply to Hale Irwin's 287, seven over par, at Winged Foot a year later when only 23 of 150 players scored lower than 75 on the first day. Tom Watson, who led after three rounds, took 79 in the last – the first of a number of missed chances.

The 25th tie in the championship's history came at Medinah in 1975, Lou Graham recovering from 11 strokes behind after 36 holes to defeat John Mahaffey, while the first Open to be held in the south, at the Atlanta AC, Georgia, in 1976, saw Jerry Pate win with a birdie on the last hole. As with Nicklaus in 1962, it was Pate's first year on the circuit. The attendance exceeded 100,000.

Lee Trevino was comparatively unknown when he won the first of his two US Open championships in 1968.

Johnny Miller seldom spares himself.

Overleaf: David Graham, of Australia, throws up his head in anguish but he still took the 1981 US Open in convincing manner.

Hubert Green had an armed guard after a death threat at Southern Hills, Oklahoma, in 1977, to win by a stroke from Lou Graham, while courage of another sort was shown by Andy North at Cherry Hills the following year. Needing a bogey five at the last, North was twice in the rough and then in a bunker. In a buffeting wind he twice had to step away from his ball before holing from four feet for the championship. Prize money rose to $330,000 at Inverness, in 1979, Hale Irwin enjoying his second success even though his last round was 75. This was the year the USGA planted a Christmas tree overnight between the first and second rounds beside the eighth tee to stop players driving down the adjacent 17th fairway, thereby shortening the hole.

All manner of records fell at Baltusrol in 1980: Nicklaus returned a total of 272 including a record-equalling first round of 63, which Tom Weiskopf matched, and also lowered the 36 and 54-hole records and joined Willie Anderson, Bobby Jones and Ben Hogan as four-time winners. The 18 years between Nicklaus' first and last victories was also the longest winning span while the Japanese Isao Aoki, who chased Nicklaus all the way and himself beat the old record, had the best finish by an Asian.

In 1981, David Graham became the first Australian to win the title playing a particularly fine last round of 67 at

Right: Hale Irwin on his way to victory at Winged Foot, New York, in 1974.

Far right: The greatest last and winning round in the US Open was Johnny Miller's 63 at Oakmont in 1973.

Bottom right: There may not be a lot of rough on American courses but there are certainly trees, as Gary Player discovers at Winged Foot in 1974.

Left: Andy North on his way to taking the US Open at Cherry Hills in 1978. He became champion again in 1985.

Overleaf: Among the features at Oakmont are the church-pew bunkers between the third and fourth holes. Arnold Palmer is trapped.

Merion. Tom Watson's elusive victory then followed in 1982 at Pebble Beach when, after an enthralling tussle with Nicklaus, he edged in front only with birdies at the last two holes, the chip he sank from off the green at the 17th hole providing one of the most dramatic moments in the history of the tournament.

Watson had an excellent chance of a successful defence at Oakmont but failed to make the most of a three-stroke lead with nine holes to play. He lost by a stroke to Larry Nelson after play was suspended overnight because of a heavy thunderstorm. They were level, Nelson

with three holes to play, Watson with four. When they resumed the following morning, Nelson played his three in par while Watson dropped a stroke.

In two years prize money had leaped from $385,000 to $600,000 at Winged Foot in 1984, the 26th tie resulting in victory for Fuzzy Zoeller over Greg Norman, of Australia. It was a popular win, remembered not only for the golf but also for Zoeller's waving of a white towel when he mistakenly thought Norman had holed for a birdie three on the last green. In fact it was only for a four which Zoeller, who was waiting on the fairway, then matched for a tie.

Above: Tom Watson 'takes off' after holing his chip for a two at Pebble Beach's 17th hole in the final round of the 1982 US Open which he went on to win.

Opposite: Isao Aoki, of Japan, played marvellously at Baltusrol in 1980 with three 68s and a 70. But it was not enough to stop Jack Nicklaus.

The American PGA

Of the four major championships, the American PGA is, in terms of longevity, senior to the Masters but junior to both the British and US Opens. It is nevertheless the second oldest event on the US tour, first being played in 1916, the year that the Professional Golfers' Association of America was formed. Its champions received a life-time exemption from all tournament pre-qualifying and this gave it a definite status symbol among the players. But for all that, the championship lacks the world-wide glamour and prestige of the other three majors; it also does not include amateurs.

One thing in the PGA's favour in its early years, however, was that it was a match-play event. This is a form of golf very popular at club level, but not with modern professionals, who regard it as unfair to complete a round of 68 and perhaps lose while another man may go round in 73 and win. They also dislike playing more than 18 holes in a day, which match-play invariably involves, and, perhaps most important of all today, it is not liked by television since there is never a guarantee of where a match will finish. It was therefore the decision, in 1958, to change to stroke-play over 72 holes that was responsible for the PGA losing the one ingredient that set it apart, though a more settled date in the calendar (for a time it clashed with the British Open) has helped its cause.

Walter Hagen was the first American-born player to win the PGA in 1921, following Jim Barnes (1916 and 1919) and Jock Hutchison (1920) who were both British-born, though resident in the States. Hagen's victory provided the beginning of a golden era. In seven years he triumphed five times, including four in a row from 1924, and Sarazen twice.

Match-play brings different demands to stroke-play for though there is a theory that one should go out with a mind just to playing the course, a careful eye must be kept on the opponent. There are times to gamble just as there are times to play safe. It was an arena to which Hagen was well suited. The flamboyance of his manner, acceptance of bad shots (he once said that he expected to hit no more than two or three exactly as intended in any one round) and uncanny short game were enough to intimidate most of his contemporaries.

Twice already US Open champion, Hagen's first win was at Inwood, New York, where he defeated the persistent Barnes, who had been in three of the four finals. Hagen did not defend at Oakmont in 1922 and Sarazen, who a month earlier had won the US Open at the tender age of 20, completed the double by defeating Emmet French. He was also too good for Hagen at Pelham, New York, in 1923, though only just, for an epic encounter between the two best golfers in America at that time resulted in Sarazen winning at the 38th, the first time the final had gone to extra holes.

There then began Hagen's historic run of four successive championships – at French Lick, Indiana, where he beat Barnes in the final, at Olympia Fields, Illinois, where he defeated 'Wild Bill' Melhorn, at Salisbury, New York, where he swept aside Leo Diegel and at Cedar Crest, Texas, where he came from behind before narrowly getting the better of Joe Turnesa.

Hagen's run came to an end at Baltimore, Maryland, in 1928 when he lost in the third round to Diegel. Hagen had then gone 22 consecutive matches without defeat and had become so used to being champion that he said he had mislaid the trophy, leaving it, he thought, in a taxicab! It was recovered however and Diegel took it home with him, having gone on to beat Sarazen, by nine and eight, and Al Espinosa, in the final, by six and five. All matches in those days were over 36 holes and the stymie was still all part of the game. It assisted Diegel to a second consecutive victory at Hillcrest, California, as John Farrell twice cannoned his ball into Diegel's, accidentally knocking it into the hole.

Match-play is somehow more susceptible to unusual incident and after intervening victories by Tommy Armour, against Sarazen, and Tom Creavy, who previously caddied for Sarazen, one of the most astonishing recoveries took place during an early round at Keller, Minnesota, in 1932. Al Watrous was nine up with only 12 holes to play against Bobby Cruickshank and in a moment of pity gave his opponent a putt that, if missed, would have put Watrous 10 up. It was generosity he was to regret. Cruickshank fought back to win, though he got no further than the semi-finals and Olin Dutra took the title.

Gene Sarazen's third and last victory followed at Blue Mound, Wisconsin, while in 1936 and 1937 Densmore Shute

became the last man to win the title in successive years, first at Pinehurst, North Carolina, and then at Pittsburgh. Sam Snead, who was subsequently to win the PGA three times, made an inauspicious first appearance in the final in 1938 at Shawnee, Pennsylvania, losing by eight and seven to Paul Runyan. Snead was also in the final two years later but lost again, this time to Byron Nelson at Hershey, Pennsylvania.

These were nevertheless good times for the PGA with Nelson becoming very much the man of the moment. He was in five finals out of six between 1939 and 1945 (no championship in 1943) winning twice. Snead won at last, at Seaview, New Jersey, in 1942 and immediately after the war came Ben Hogan, whose PGA victory at Portland, Oregon, in 1946 was his first major championship. Three down after 18 holes in the final to Porky Oliver, Hogan still won by six and four, having played the first nine holes after lunch in 30. Two years later, after Jim Ferrier had become the first Australian to win, Hogan triumphed again at Norwood Hills, Missouri, having just taken the US Open for the first time.

Snead, his great rival, then struck again, first in his native state of Virginia at the Hermitage club in 1949 and again at Oakmont in 1951.

The best recovery in a final came from Walter Burkemo at Birmingham, Michigan, in 1953. Seven down at lunch, he recovered to beat Felice Tarza by two and one. But with six former champions beaten in the first two rounds, the championship suffered and for the first time thoughts turned towards stroke-play. The step was taken in 1958 and Dow Finsterwald, who had lost the previous year in the final to Lionel Hebert, got his revenge with a two-stroke victory at Llanarch, Pennsylvania.

Arnold Palmer looked as if he might win at Firestone, Ohio, in 1960 but failed to capitalize on an opening round of 67 and the title went instead to Jay Hebert, brother of Lionel. It was to prove a championship always to elude Palmer, for all his power. Yet power is not everything. Jerry Barber, who triumphed at Olympia Fields, Illinois, in 1961 stood only 5ft 5in (1.65m), proving what can be done by a man with a good short game.

Walter Hagen dominated the early years of the PGA, then a match-play event, winning four times in a row.

Gary Player, of South Africa, became the first player based overseas to become PGA champion, in 1962 at Aronimink, Pennsylvania, while Jack Nicklaus, wasting no time at all, quickly added at Dallas, Texas, the PGA to the Masters he had won earlier in the year and the US Open the previous year. That made three out of the four major championships within two years of his turning professional. Palmer's frustration was meanwhile continuing. At Columbus, Ohio, in 1964, he broke 70 in every round and still only tied second with Nicklaus, three strokes behind Bobby Nichols, whose total of 271 remains a championship record.

Nicklaus was second again in 1965, this time to Dave Marr, at Laurel Valley, Pennsylvania, and then third in 1967 to Don January (who beat Don Massengale in a play-off) at Columbine, Colorado. In six starts Nicklaus had then been in the top three five times. The 50th championship, at Pecan Valley, Texas, in 1968, was marked by Julius Boros, at 48, becoming the oldest champion. Raymond Floyd and Dave Stockton suc-

ceeded him before Nicklaus won the second of his five titles in 1971 in the first championship to be held at the association's headquarters at Palm Beach, Florida. With two victories already in each of the other three major championships, Nicklaus consequently became the only man to have completed a second 'set' of the game's principal honours, a third 'set' coming later.

Player's second victory was at Oakland Hills, Michigan, in 1972 but a more historic moment still belonged to Nicklaus at Canterbury, Ohio, in 1973 when he passed Bobby Jones' haul of 13 major titles. Riding high once again, Nicklaus was second to Lee Trevino at Tanglewood, North Carolina, in 1974 and then edged closer still to Walter Hagen's record of five PGA titles with a fourth win at Firestone in 1975.

Gene Littler, whose effortless swing and courageous fight against cancer earned him a multitude of admirers, might have added the PGA to his earlier US Open victory in 1977 at Pebble Beach when he led by five strokes with nine holes to play. But he then allowed

Gary Player, who has won the American PGA twice (1962–72) has been one of the complete masters of bunker play.

Raymond Floyd's two PGA victories came 13 years apart, in 1969 at Dayton, Ohio, and at Tulsa, Oklahoma, in 1982.

Right: John Mahaffey, who beat both Jerry Pate and Tom Watson in a play-off for the 1978 PGA at Oakmont.

Right: Lanny Wadkins, who made up five strokes in nine holes to catch Gene Littler at Pebble Beach in 1977. He then won the sudden-death play-off.

Far right: Larry Nelson's first major championship victory was in the 1981 PGA at Atlanta.

Lanny Wadkins first to catch and then beat him in the first sudden-death play off to any of the four major championships.

Suddenly there was a spate of ties, John Mahaffey making up Tom Watson's four-stroke lead going into the last nine holes at Oakmont in 1978, with Jerry Pate also missing a quite short putt for victory on the 18th green. Mahaffey beat them both with a birdie at the second extra hole. Next it was the turn of David Graham, of Australia, at Oakland Hills. He got the better of Ben Crenshaw in extra time, despite Crenshaw, like Palmer before him in 1974, having broken 70 in every round.

Having set all manner of records in winning his fourth US Open at Baltusrol in 1980, Nicklaus set about some more a few months later in the PGA at Oak Hill, New York. His seven-stroke winning margin was the biggest ever and he also equalled Hagen's tally of five titles.

There was a first win for Larry Nelson at Atlanta, Georgia, in 1981, a second for

Jack Nicklaus' fifth PGA title, at Oak Hill in 1980, was also his most commanding. He won by seven strokes from Andy Bean.

Opposite: Lee Trevino was 44 when he won the PGA at Shoal Creek, Alabama, in 1985, but it was not all plain sailing.

Left: Lee Trevino (left) and Gary Player keep in step but it was Trevino who finished in front at Shoal Creek.

Below: Hal Sutton, the 1980 American Amateur champion, won the PGA in only his second year as a professional, at Riviera, California, three years later.

Raymond Floyd at Southern Hills, Oklahoma, in 1982 and a first for Hal Sutton at Riviera, California, in 1983, in only his second full season as a professional. But in 1984 it was one of the game's most popular players, Lee Trevino, who proved also his lasting qualities. Though now 44, he beat 70 in every round at Shoal Creek, Alabama, no one chasing him longer or harder than Gary Player, who was then 49 but still good enough to tie second and equal the lowest single round of 63 by Bruce Crampton in 1975.

The Masters

Although the United States Masters is regarded as one of the 'Big Four' championships, the Augusta National Club, where it is always held, make no such claim. The official title is the Masters *tournament*. Furthermore the field, which fluctuates between 70 and 80 and is therefore half the size of that in the US Open, British Open or American PGA, is strictly speaking invitational. Certainly those invitations are now by qualification, but the club's organizing committee reserves the right of having the final word.

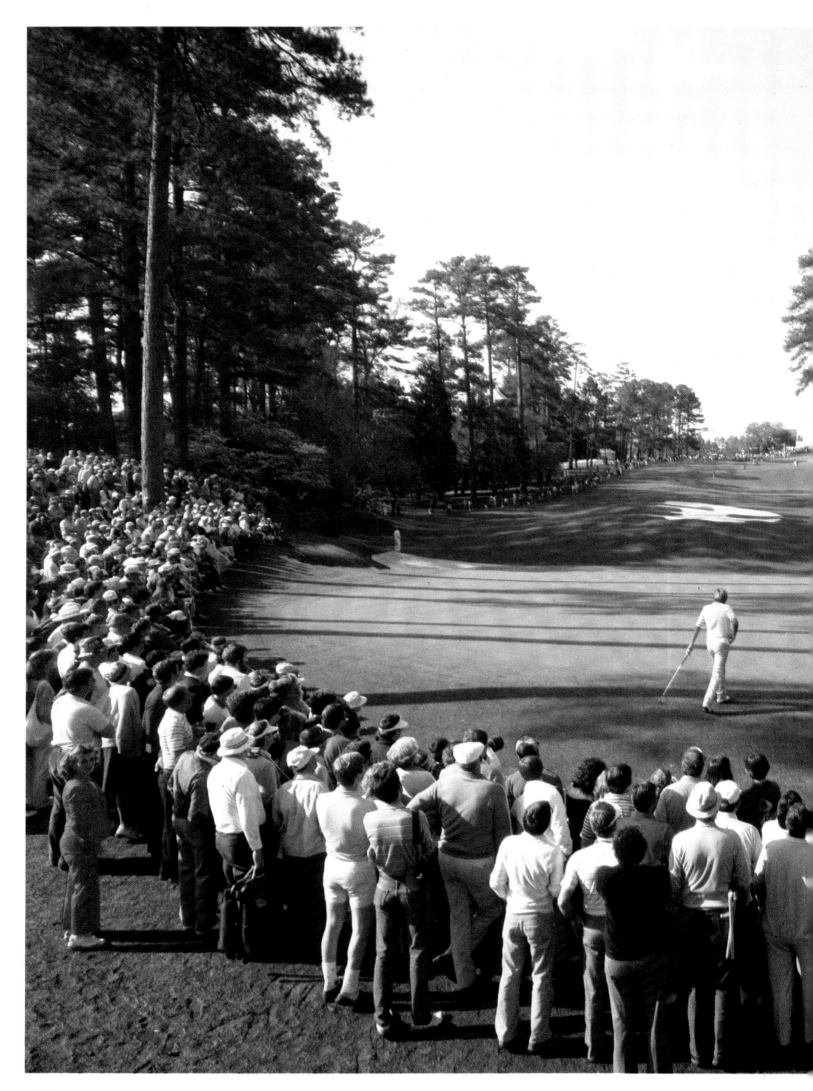

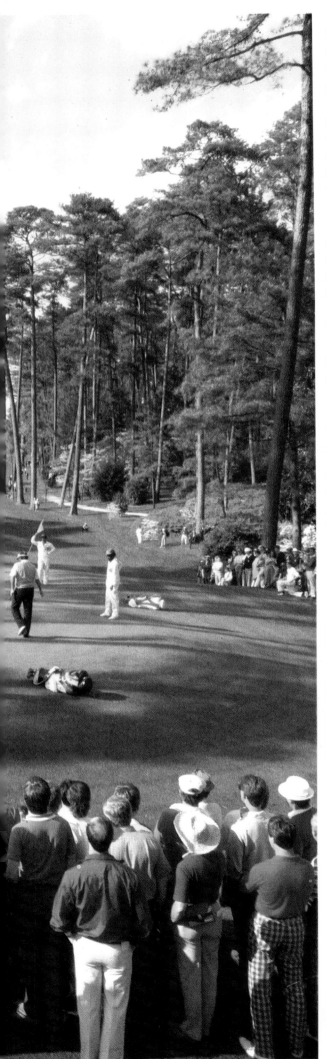

It is above all a tournament requiring high standards, first set by Bobby Jones, who helped Alister Mackenzie design the course and became club president in perpetuity. After the death of Jones in 1971, Clifford Roberts, the club chairman, continued to run the tournament with an iron fist and his successors have since made few concessions. In some respects the Masters has not moved with the times but there remains a charm and magic about it that is unique.

Such has been public demand that admission has long since been by advance ticket sales only, most people returning year after year. There is no advertising on the course and the programme is a single sheet of paper with starting times on one side, a map of the course on the other and a gentle reminder, written by Jones, 'not to applaud any misplays'. Players go out in twos rather than threes, there is always a good sprinkling of amateurs, including the British Amateur champion, and representation from overseas.

There are a number of private dinners before the tournament, including one hosted by the reigning champion for all past champions. These champions have their own locker room, which is out of bounds to anyone else other than by invitation. At the conclusion of the

Opposite: The 10th green at Augusta National.

Below: A presentation by the British press to Clifford Roberts (centre), chairman of Augusta National, in 1977. Left to right: Dai Davies, Donald Steel, Henry Longhurst, Peter Ryde, Peter Dobereiner, Eric Humphreys, Roberts, Ron Fox, Renton Laidlaw, Michael McDonnell, the author, Pat Ward-Thomas and Dudley Doust.

Right: A moment Gary Player can hardly have expected. He had six birdies in the last nine holes in 1978 and won after being seven strokes behind going into the last round.

Opposite: The final drive, Ben Crenshaw on the 18th tee in 1984.

tournament the winner is made an honorary member of Augusta National and as such is entitled to wear the club's distinctive green blazer, into which he is assisted by the previous champion at a special ceremony on the lawns sweeping down to the course.

The television company which covers the tournament has a specific list of do's and don'ts. When one commentator remarked in a moment of excitement 'look at the mob running', the programme director was hauled before the committee the following day and told forcefully that 'Augusta National does not have mobs and they certainly do not run'.

Such is the attention to detail that scarcely a year goes by when some alteration is not made to the course: a new bunker here, some trees there or a green relaid and once, in 1981, the whole lot relaid with bentgrass rather than the previous Bermuda. There is no such thing as a bad lie at Augusta. Green-coloured sand conceals old divots, the water hazards are dyed blue and, as the tournament is scheduled to coincide with the many shrubs coming into full bloom, the whole scene, under clear Georgia skies, is a picture.

Jones himself played in the first Masters in 1934, even though he had retired from competitive golf four years

earlier. Horton Smith won but it was the following year that the tournament caught on, all as a result of just one stroke. Gene Sarazen was three behind Craig Wood, who was already in the clubhouse, when he came to the par five 15th in the last round. But he made an albatross (double eagle) two by holing a four-wood shot from more than 200yd (182m) across the water in front of the green. It enabled him to tie and the following day he won the 36-hole play-off.

There was a fine recovery, too, in 1936 as Horton Smith became champion for the second time by making up six strokes on Harry Cooper, while in 1937 Byron Nelson enjoyed a six-stroke swing in the space of two holes against Ralph Guldahl, who was leading at the time. Nelson had a two at the short 12th and then an eagle three at the 13th, whereas Guldahl went 5, 6. Such catastrophies have always been a feature at Augusta where five holes on the inward half are threatened by water.

Guldahl was pipped again in 1938, this time by Henry Picard, but it proved to be third time lucky for him 12 months later when he played the last nine holes in 33 to edge past Sam Snead, who had looked a sure winner. Jimmy Demaret and Craig Wood were the champions in 1940 and 1941 respectively but it was Byron Nelson's victory in 1942, the last Masters until after the war, that typified the many great tussles at Augusta.

It was Nelson's second win and it came after a tie with Ben Hogan, who had been eight strokes behind after 36 holes. Hogan then led by three after five holes of the play-off but though he played the next 11 in one under par, Nelson still overtook him with what he described as the best spell of golf of his career, finishing in 69 to Hogan's 70.

Hogan was runner-up again in 1946, this time to Herman Keiser and once more by a single stroke after both had taken three putts on the last green. Demaret then emulated Horton Smith and Byron Nelson as two-time winners,

The sun does not always shine at Augusta.

Gene Sarazen, whose double eagle (albatross) two at the 15th hole in 1935 helped to make the Masters famous.

Sam Snead, three times
Masters champion
between 1949 and 1954.

with an amateur, Frank Stranahan, equal second. No amateur has ever won the Masters but Ken Venturi (1956) and Charlie Coe (1961) were both runners-up, while in 1954 Billy Joe Patton led with six holes to play before finishing a stroke behind Hogan and Snead.

Claude Harmon equalled the record of 279 in 1948, and a year later Snead, having played the first two rounds in 73, 75, finished with two successive 67s to win the Masters at last, not looking back from the moment he holed a chip at the 12th for a four after putting his tee shot in the water and mis-hitting the next into long grass.

This was the beginning of some golden years at Augusta for in 1950 Demaret came from nowhere over the last six holes to beat Jim Ferrier and become the first triple champion. The next four Masters were dominated by Hogan and Snead, both of them winning twice in alternate years. Hogan's last round 68 in 1951 was said not to have contained a single error of shot judgment or execution; while in 1952 Snead, having taken the lead with 70, 67, then took 77, 72 in some very high winds but still finished four strokes clear.

Then it was Hogan's turn again in 1953, his three rounds in the 60s and a total of 274 breaking the record by five strokes. It was the same year in which he went on to take both the US and British Opens but his golf at Augusta he judged to have been as good as at any time in his career.

The intense rivalry between Hogan and Snead came to a head in 1954 when they tied on 289 after a major scare from the then little-known amateur, Billy Joe Patton. The play-off attracted unusually big crowds, as was to be expected when the two best golfers were in confrontation. Nor were they disappointed, Snead winning by a stroke, 70 against 71. By contrast Dr Cary Middlecoff had seven strokes to spare over Hogan in 1955, a record margin that was under some threat a year later.

It came from an unlikely source since it was the amateur, Ken Venturi, who stood four strokes clear with 18 holes to play. Middlecoff, the defending champion, was closest to him but nerves got the better of Venturi, who had a last round of 80, and it was Jack Burke junior, eight strokes behind going into those last 18 holes, who came through to snatch the title with a final round of 71.

There was another recovery in 1957 as Doug Ford, three strokes behind Snead, stormed through with a last round of 66. Prize money was then, at $53,000, almost double what it was in the US Open and the upsurge of public interest accelerated further with the first of Arnold Palmer's four victories in 1958. At 28, Palmer was the youngest champion since Nelson, who was 25 when he won in 1937.

Palmer had a magnetism about him and a year later he was sharing the lead again after three rounds with the Canadian, Stan Leonard. But Art Wall overtook them both with a concluding 66 that included five birdies in the last six holes. Yet it was Palmer's birdie, birdie, finish to beat Ken Venturi, now a professional, in 1960 that caught the imagination of the golfing world. As with Severiano Ballesteros 20 years later, Palmer was at his most formidable on Augusta's broad fairways and he very nearly became the first man to win two years running. Instead the title went abroad for the first time, in the hands of Gary Player. A stroke behind Palmer as he came to the 18th hole, Player got down in two from a greenside bunker for his four while Palmer, from the same place, took a six.

Both were also involved in a tight finish in 1962, Player, Palmer and Dow Finsterwald all tieing on 280 for the first three-way play-off. Player was three strokes ahead at the turn, but Palmer mounted one of his familiar 'charges' and came home in 31 for a 68 that left both his rivals stranded.

Art Wall, one of the most enduring players in the Masters. He won the title in 1959.

Right: The 16th green at Augusta National.

Below: Billy Casper receives a standing ovation as he reaches the 18th green for victory in 1970 from Gary Player, who keeps a respectful distance.

Nicklaus joins in

Jack Nicklaus, in only his second year as a professional, won the first of his five Masters in 1963, just a stroke ahead of Tony Lema, who was making his first appearance. For the most part the weather was rough and the scoring high, but as the sun shone the following year so Palmer gained a then record fourth victory in the space of seven years. Again he was under 70 in three of the four rounds and only Nicklaus and Dave Marr were within six strokes of him.

In 1965 the roles were reversed, Nicklaus winning by nine strokes from Palmer and Player with a record 271 (67, 71, 64, 69). This was three strokes inside Hogan's previous best, in 1953. It was an exhibition of golf that drew from Jones the comment: 'Mr Nicklaus plays a game with which I am not familiar'. A year later Nicklaus became the first man successfully to defend the title, surviving a tie with Tommy Jacobs and Gay Brewer after no less than 17 players had held or shared the lead. In five years as a professional, Nicklaus had already won the Masters three times.

Brewer had quick compensation for his near miss by becoming champion in 1967 when his thrilling last round of 67 proved just too much for Bobby Nichols. Then in 1968 Bob Goalby finished with a 66 to stay a stroke ahead of Roberto de Vicenzo, with whom he had been tied after three rounds. It was however a tragic disappointment for de Vicenzo. The popular Argentine, on his 45th birthday, was robbed of a tie only on a technicality. He had in fact scored a last round of 65, giving him a total of 277, the same as Goalby. In his excitement, however, he failed to notice that his marker had put him down for a four at the 17th when in fact he had had a birdie three. He signed the card and it was only later that the error was discovered. In such circumstances the score must stand for the player, not the marker, is responsible for a card's accuracy. Though every avenue was explored to find some sort of loophole, the Rules of Golf had to apply. Typically, Vicenzo merely commented: 'What a silly I am'.

After 25 players had either led or jointly led in 1969, the tallest of them, George Archer, who stood 6ft 6in (1.98m), overtook Billy Casper. Not for the first time, a near miss one year was followed by victory the next, Casper winning in 1970 after a tie with Gene Littler, the sixth play-off so far. Bert Yancey (who was so obsessed with Augusta National that he built a model of the course to study at home) and Player were both involved in a fluctuating last round but Casper was always in control of the play-off.

Two birdies in the last four holes enabled Charles Coody to break clear of Nicklaus and Johnny Miller in 1971 but the inevitable figure of Nicklaus was there again in 1972 as he equalled Palmer's four victories. For ten years the tournament had been blessed with glorious weather, but in 1973 rain forced the final round to be played on the Monday for the first time, when there was also the prospect of a British winner in Peter Oosterhuis. He led by three strokes going into the last round but a 74 relegated him to a share of third place as Tommy Aaron came from four strokes behind with a final 68.

Gary Player won his second Masters in 1974 after eight players had been in contention going into the last nine holes. But that engendered nothing like the

Peter Oosterhuis, of Britain, held a three-stroke lead going into the final round in 1973 but in the end could only share third place behind Tommy Aaron.

excitement the following year as Nicklaus made history with his record fifth victory after a marvellous tussle with Johnny Miller and Tom Weiskopf. Nicklaus had a last round of 68 to overtake Weiskopf (70) while Miller's 66 was a brilliant effort. Indeed both Miller and Weiskopf, the latter runner-up for a fourth time, missed birdie putts on the last green to force a play-off.

Opening rounds of 65, 66, launched Raymond Floyd to a most impressive victory in his 12th Masters in 1976 as he tied the record of 271 set by Nicklaus 11 years earlier. He won by eight strokes from Ben Crenshaw after building his victory around the four par fives. In the first three rounds, invariably using a four wood for his approaches, he played them in 11 under par – ten birdies and one par.

Tom Watson's two great confrontations with Nicklaus in 1977 began at Augusta as they slugged it out shot for shot over the last 18 holes, Nicklaus making up a three-stroke deficit to be level with five to play. But Watson sank a big putt for a three at the 17th on the way to a 67 while Nicklaus, gambling on a three at the last, took five and finished two strokes adrift. Three months later Watson prevailed again in another clash between the two at the British Open at Turnberry.

No one gave Gary Player a thought when the last round began in 1978. He was, after all, 42, his first Masters victory had been 17 years before and he was seven strokes behind Hubert Green as he came to the ninth hole. But a birdie there was the first of seven in the last ten holes and his 64 brought him an astonishing third Masters as well as his ninth major championship. Watson and Rod Funseth might both have tied but the best

Jack Nicklaus makes the champion's speech after winning the 1975 Masters by a stroke from Johnny Miller (leaning forward) and Tom Weiskopf. Gary Player is seated left.

In 1976 Raymond Floyd equalled Jack Nicklaus' record total of 271, which had been set 11 years earlier.

chance was missed by Green. He failed to hole a putt of a yard on the last green that would have put him in a play-off. It left Player as the oldest Masters champion.

Fuzzy Zoeller had the distinction of becoming the first (other than Horton Smith in the tournament's inaugural year) to win the Masters at his first attempt in 1979. He beat Watson and Ed Sneed in a play-off, reduced now to sudden death, at the second extra hole. However it was a victory very much by courtesy of Sneed, who held a three-stroke lead with only three holes to play.

At such moments the nerves have a habit of playing up and Sneed's three successive bogeys will be likely to haunt him all his life.

In the summer of 1979 Severiano Ballesteros, of Spain, charted an erratic course to his first victory in the British Open at Royal Lytham. In the spring of 1980 he charted a most meticulous one in adding to it his first Masters. He dominated with each one of his first three rounds under 70 (66, 69, 68) and then an outward 33 on the final day. He was at that point 16 under par and needed only two more birdies to break the record. But

Fuzzy Zoeller, the first sudden-death winner of the Masters, in 1979.

Ed Sneed can hardly believe it as his putt to win the 1979 Masters stops on the edge of the hole. He had led by three strokes with three holes to play. Then he lost the play-off.

Jack Nicklaus may have won the Masters five times but sometimes life gets very difficult, as here at the 15th.

a ten-stroke lead suddenly dwindled only to two as error followed error. Ballesteros had to take a firm grip on himself before playing the last five holes in one under par to become the first European champion. He was also, at 23, the youngest.

Nicklaus seemed destined for a sixth victory in 1981 when he played the first two rounds in 70 and 65. However in the space of 12 holes in the third round he slipped from four strokes ahead to four behind and it was Watson who saw the chance and took it. As in 1977, there were two strokes between them, Johnny Miller putting in another late burst (68) to tie second.

Craig Stadler had some alarming moments before he beat Dan Pohl at the first extra hole of a sudden-death play-off in 1982. He had led by six strokes with nine holes to play but took four bogeys at the last seven for a 73. Pohl's 67 therefore gave him a second chance, though he could not take it.

Having won from the front in 1980, Ballesteros took his second Masters from behind in 1983. Going into Monday's final round, bad weather having intervened, the Spaniard stood a stroke behind the formidable trio of Watson, Stadler and Floyd, each past champions and now sharing the lead. But an eagle and two birdies from Ballesteros in the first four holes spectacularly put them all to flight. Instead it was Ben Crenshaw and Tom Kite who made up ground to tie second, four strokes back.

Again, however, the runner-up one year was champion the next and seldom has there been a more popular one than Crenshaw in 1984. Over the years he had three times been runner-up in the Masters (1976–78–83), twice in the British Open (1978–79), once in the PGA (when in 1979 he lost in a play-off) while in the US Open of 1975 he tied third, though only a stroke behind Lou Graham and John Mahaffey, who had to play off. Now all that was forgotten as some brilliant putting in the final round brought him victory by two strokes from Tom Watson. No man has been more relieved, nor more proud.

Overleaf: Severiano Ballesteros chips into the hole at the 18th for his four to make sure of his second Masters in 1983.

3 THE GREAT PLAYERS

Severiano Ballesteros
Born Pedrena, Spain, 9 April 1957. Open champion 1979–84. Masters champion 1980–83. World match-play champion 1981–82–84. Ryder Cup 1979–83.

His first golf clubs were sticks he found on the beach along the Bay of Santander, close to where he was born. His elder brothers had given him the head of an old three iron, its shaft long since broken. With all the invention of youth, he would jam the end of a stick into the hosel, soak it in a bucket of water overnight so that the wood swelled and in the morning he would have a golf club. At least, it was a golf club of sorts.

When the stick broke he would find another; and repeat the process. He had no golf balls; instead he would use the roundest stones he could find. He would dig his own holes, plan his own course. The names of Nicklaus and Palmer meant nothing to him. He was too young.

But as his frame filled and he graduated to clubs of his own and even a proper golf ball, the hours he had spent alone on the beach with his imagination brought untold benefit. He could do more with a three iron than most can do with a full set of 14 clubs and his uncle, the gifted Ramon Sota, would nod his head wisely and say to anyone who would listen: 'Just wait. My nephew, Severiano Ballesteros. He will be the best'.

Just how good, even Sota may not have realized. When Seve, as he became known, burst upon the world scene he did so without warning, in the Open championship of 1976, at Royal Birkdale. He was 19, still in only his third year as a tournament player; but for three rounds he led Johnny Miller and faltered only in the final round to tie second with Nicklaus.

There was, however, an invigorating abandon about his game that at once caught the imagination. Within another three years he was Open champion, the first Continental to win the oldest and most coveted title in the world since Arnaud Massy, of France, in 1907. A year later, in 1980, he became the first European and only the second non-American to win the Masters.

By then he had been leading money winner in Europe for three successive years (1976–78) and had spread his wings far across the globe in his hunt for international titles: in France, Holland, Japan, Kenya, Germany, Scandinavia, Switzerland, Australia, Ireland, New Zealand and, of course, back in his native Spain.

Ballesteros became the most marketable golfer since Palmer, with whom many would draw a parallel for attacking instincts. Tall, dark and handsome, his natural strength needed some curbing but he has always been the possessor of a wonderful short game with the remarkable knack of getting himself out of apparently hopeless trouble.

The Latin blood within him made him a difficult man to handle, particularly as he fought for his rights to appearance money on the European tour. He also showed reluctance to join the American tour full time. But subsequent victories in the Masters again in 1983 and the Open a second time at St. Andrews in 1984 were almost inevitable.

There is a joyous vigour about Severiano Ballesteros in full flight.

'Big Momma', as JoAnne Carner is affectionately known, holes another putt.

JoAnne Carner
Born Kirkland, Washington, 4 April 1939.
US Women's Open champion 1971–76. US Women's amateur champion 1957–60–62–66–68. Curtis Cup 1958–60–62–64.

JoAnne Carner is one of the few golfers who have enjoyed two nicknames during their careers. An an amateur, when her maiden name was Gunderson, she was known as 'the Great Gundy'; as a professional she has come to be referred to as 'Big Momma'.

Both reflect her popularity and also a strong physique which enables her to hit the ball 'like a man', her swing being much more curtailed than those of most women golfers. An extrovert personality, she was blessed with powerful legs and wrists, further strengthened by intense physical training.

Curiously, she has never been a great practiser, having great faith in the fact that everything would fall into place as soon as she stepped on to the first tee. Formidable in match-play, she turned professional at the comparatively advanced age of 30, seeking new challenges as much as anything.

As an amateur, Mrs Carner made more impact than anyone since Babe Zaharias, another long hitter. She won a record five American amateur championships, her first at the age of 18, the youngest since Beatrice Hoyt, in 1896. She is also the last Amateur to have won an LPGA event, the Burdine's Invitational in Miami in 1969, which influenced her decision to turn professional. Justification was not long in coming; she won another tournament in her rookie year and the first two US Opens 12 months after that. Since then she has become the most dominant figure in American women's golf.

In 15 years Mrs Carner has won 40 tournaments and in 1982 became only the tenth player to be elected to the LPGA Hall of Fame – an honour bestowed only on those who have won 30 tour events and two majors, 35 events and one major or 40 LPGA tournaments. Patty Berg, Betty Jameson, Louise Suggs, Babe Zaharias, Betsy Rawls, Mickey Wright, Kathy Whitworth, Sandra Haynie and Carol Mann are the others.

Mrs Carner became a dollar millionaire in 1981 and her career earnings now approach $2 million, an all-time record. She has won the Vare Trophy for the lowest stroke average of the year five times and Rolex Player of the Year (for the most top five finishes in any one season) three times.

In 1981 she became only the fifth woman to receive the Bob Jones Award, which is given annually by the USGA to the person who, 'by a single act or over the years, emulates Bob Jones' sportsmanship, respect for the game and its rules, generosity of spirit, sense of fair play, self control and perhaps even sacrifice'.

Henry Cotton

Born London, 26 January 1907. Open champion 1934–37–38. Ryder Cup 1929–37–47 (non-playing captain 1953).

Americans first dominated the Open championship between 1924 and 1933 when it was won three times each by Bobby Jones, the amateur, and Walter Hagen and once by Jim Barnes, Tommy Armour, Gene Sarazen and Densmore Shute. It took Henry Cotton to stop them.

His victory by five strokes at Royal St. George's, Sandwich, in 1934 was notable for his opening rounds of 67 and 65, the second of which gave the name to the famous Dunlop '65' ball, and he was so far ahead after three rounds that he was able to take 79 for the last and still not be threatened.

If this final round revealed a highly strung disposition, Cotton was nevertheless master of his nerves, as he proved three years later when he outpaced the whole of the visiting American Ryder Cup team in winning the Open for a second time at Carnoustie.

The untimely outbreak of war in 1939, just as he was in his golfing prime, almost certainly robbed him of other championship victories. However after being invalided out of the RAF he helped to raise considerable sums for the Red Cross, for which he was made an MBE. He was also still good enough, at the age of 41, to win the Open a third time at Muirfield in 1948. No other British golfer has been so dominant since the days of Vardon, Braid and Taylor at the turn of the century.

His mastery of the game came less from any natural gifts as from sheer hard work. Many were the times when he practised long after the sun had gone down and his hands bled. But his dedication had its rewards and a sharp intellect enabled him not only to understand the technicalities of the swing better than most but also to upgrade golf as a profession.

Driven on by his devoted Argentine-born wife, Toots, he mixed easily with millionaires and princes who, at a golf school he set up in Monte Carlo, drove brand new golf balls out to sea. He even appeared in the same London theatre production as Nellie Wallace, giving an exhibition using luminous golf balls on a darkened stage.

Three times British match-play champion and winner of many continental championships, Cotton made three Ryder Cup appearances and was also a non-playing captain. At the age of 49 he was sixth in the Open at Hoylake and made his last appearance at Turnberry in 1977, aged 70.

An author of a number of books, Cotton also designed several golf courses, his favourite undoubtedly being Penina, on the Portuguese Algarve, where he has spent much of the evening of a full and colourful life.

Henry Cotton, three times British Open champion.

Walter Hagen, in his prime years of the 1920s.

Walter Hagen
Born Rochester, New York, 21 December 1892. Died 1969. Open champion 1922–24–28–29. US Open champion 1914–19. American PGA champion 1921–24–25–26–27. Ryder Cup 1927–29–31–33–35 (non-playing captain 1937).

Walter Hagen was, in every sense, a golfing pioneer. After his second victory in the US Open, in 1919, he became the first purely tournament professional, dispensing with the then usual practice for golfers to have a club attachment. He also took the game out of Norfolk jackets and breeches into pullovers and cardigans of attractive colours, off-set by two-tone shoes.

But Hagen did much more than that. He had, he often said, no wish to be a millionaire, only the desire to live like one, which he did. He was consequently responsible almost single-handed for demolishing the social barrier that then existed between the professionals and the amateurs.

When he crossed the Atlantic to compete in his first Open, at Deal in 1920, he found that professionals were not allowed into the clubhouse. So Hagen hired a Rolls Royce and a butler and lunched on caviar, smoked salmon and champagne outside the main entrance. At Troon in 1923, when similar restrictions were still in force, he declined to enter the clubhouse for the prize presentation after finishing second to Arthur Havers and instead invited spectators for a drink at the inn where he had been staying.

The Americans were the first to recognize professionals as equals and when, in 1920, the Inverness, Ohio, club opened wide it doors, it was Hagen who organized a collection for a presentation grandfather clock, which still stands in the club's main hallway.

Hagen was as flamboyant on the course as he was off it. His relaxed manner as he chatted happily to spectators between strokes frequently unnerved his opponents and he regarded no shot as impossible. Consequently he was probably at his best at match-play, as his four consecutive triumphs in the American PGA when he won 22 successive games, all of them over 36 holes, prove.

Hagen did nothing by halves. in 1928 he played the Briton Archie Compston in one of the then popular challenge matches and lost by 18 and 17. Totally undeterred, he went straight to Sandwich for the Open and won it for the third time, beating Gene Sarazen by two strokes and Compston by three.

After finishing 53rd in his first Open in 1920, he was first four times, second once and third once in his next seven attempts. Yet he never expected to hit more than two or three perfect strokes in any one round. Instead he was a master at turning three shots into two around the greens, being a particularly deadly putter.

A member of the first two American teams that played, and lost to, Britain in unofficial international matches in 1921 and 1926, Hagen played in the first five Ryder Cup encounters and lost only one of nine games. In 1937 he was also the first American to captain a winning team on British soil.

Ben Hogan

Born Dublin, Texas, 13 August 1912.
Open champion 1953. US Open champion 1948–50–51–53. Masters champion 1951–53. American PGA champion 1946–48. Ryder Cup 1947–51 (non-playing captain 1949–67).

Ben Hogan is the only man to have won the Masters, US Open and British Open in the same year, 1953. No one else has come as close to completing the Grand Slam, and Hogan perhaps only failed because he was unable to get back from Britain, where at Carnoustie he had made his solitary Open championship appearance, in time to compete in the American PGA.

There is no telling as to whether Hogan would have succeeded or failed to add the fourth title; but there is no doubt that he was the best-equipped golfer of his time, and even all-time. Never has the mantle, 'a legend in his own lifetime' been more appropriate.

In many ways the legend began on 2 February 1949, on Highway 80 between Fort Worth and Van Horn in Texas on a fog-shrouded morning when Hogan's car collided head on with a bus. He nearly died, but even so lay cruelly injured, with mangled legs trapped in the wreckage for 90 minutes before he was gently born away to hospital and major surgery.

It was doubted that Hogan would ever walk again, let alone play golf. He did both, becoming an even greater golfer than before the accident. Though unable to play for the remainder of 1949, he filed an 'experimental' entry to the Los Angeles Open the following January and promptly tied with Sam Snead before losing the play-off. The same year he won the US Open at Merion, painfully surviving five rounds after another tie.

Before his accident, Hogan had won the US Open once, in 1948, and the PGA twice, in 1946 and 1948. After it, he won the US Open three times (1950–51–53), the Masters twice (1951–53) and that British Open in 1953. With Gene Sarazen, Jack Nicklaus and Gary Player, he is one of the only players to have triumphed in all four of these major championships.

Yet it took him years of hard work, even before his car crash. He was 25 before he won his first tournament and 33 before he collected his first major title, the PGA in 1946. By degrees however he acquired what is commonly regarded as the 'perfect' swing. 'No one ever covered the flag like Hogan', it was said.

There was a total ruthlessness about his game that set him apart. He would practise for hours and, even in his later years, when he walked on to the practice ground at a tournament it was common for all the other players to stop and simply watch.

His closing 67 in the 1951 US Open at Oakland Hills as he 'brought this monster to its knees' and hi clinical destruction of Carnoustie as, after two weeks of intense study, he returned 73, 71, 70 and 68, were just two of his finest hours. His consistency was also mirrored in the fact that in 14 consecutive US Opens and 14 consecutive Masters he was never out of the first 10 and 18 times in the first four.

Ben Hogan in 1953, the year he won the British and US Opens and the Masters.

Bobby Jones in his 1930 Grand Slam year.

Bobby Jones

Born Atlantia, Georgia 17 March 1902. Died 1971.
Open champion 1926–27–30.
Amateur champion 1930.
US Open champion 1923–26–29–30.
US Amateur champion 1924–25–27–28–30.
Walker Cup 1922–24–26–28–30.

No man can be more than the greatest golfer of his time, but Robert Tyre Jones junior, better known as 'Bobby' (though in fact his own preference was 'Bob'), was unquestionably the greatest amateur golfer of all time. He was a sporting hero as much as he was a golfing hero and when, in 1930, he returned to America having won both Britain's Open and Amateur championships, it was to a ticker-tape reception in New York.

He went on that summer to win both the US Open and the US Amateur, each for the fourth time, and thus completed in a single year what Jones regarded as the 'Impregnable Quadrilateral'. The golfing world dubbed it the Grand Slam. It was a feat that, it is safe to say, will never be repeated.

Jones at once retired, still only 28. Though the supreme champion with a style that came straight out of the textbooks, eight years of championship-winning golf had taken a severe toll. Often he would lose a stone (14lb/6.3kg) in weight during one event while he frequently had to forego the custom of wearing a neck-tie on the course for fear that it would make him physically sick.

Yet such was his mastery of both himself and the game that for eight years, beginning in 1923 when he won the US Open at Inwood, New York, after a play-off with Bobby Cruickshank, Jones was well nigh invincible. In that time he won 13 of what were then regarded as the major championships before the Masters and the American PGA replaced the amateur championships of Britain and America as Grand Slam targets.

In addition to his four US Open victories between 1920 and 1930, Jones was second four times and on the other occasions fifth, eighth and 11th. With his trusty Calamity Jane putter, his average winning match-play margin in his five successful US Amateur championships was nine and eight (over 36 holes) while in five Walker Cup matches against Britain he had an average of eight and seven.

Jones was as popular in Britain as he was in America and when, in 1958, he captained the United States in the inaugural world amateur team championship for the Eisenhower trophy, he was given the Freedom of the Burgh of St. Andrews in a moving ceremony at the university.

The famous Old course had become his favourite, one on which he had finally triumphed in the 1930 Amateur championship on the way to his Grand Slam, though on his first appearance there in 1921 he had torn up his card in frustration.

A highly educated man, with degrees in literature, law and engineering, Jones was the inspiration of the Masters tournament at Augusta National on a course he helped design. His final years were tormented by an agonizing muscular debilitation, which he bore as gracefully as he did his many triumphs.

Bobby Locke

**Born Germiston, Transvaal,
20 November 1917.
Open champion 1949–50–52–57.
South African Open champion
1935–37–38–39–40–46–50–51–55.**

Bobby (christened Arthur d'Arcy by his Irish parents) Locke stands alongside Gary Player as one of the two greatest products of South African golf. He was the first man to win the British Open four times since the days of Vardon, Braid and Taylor around the turn of the century, though subsequently he was overtaken by both the Australian, Peter Thomson, and the American, Tom Watson.

It was unfortunate that Locke's supremacy came at a time when American interest in the Open championship had not yet been revived, for he had already proved himself in the States as well. He had been persuaded to go there by Sam Snead, whom he had beaten 12 times in a series of 16 challenge matches in South Africa.

Although he stayed for only two seasons, due to an incompatability with Americans as a whole, they were nevertheless littered with success. In 1947 he played in 13 stroke-play tournaments, won six, was runner-up in two more and never finished lower than seventh. In 1948, he played 25 tournaments, won two, finished second in another two and was in the top ten in all but three of the rest.

But his disenchantment with American golf drove him across the Atlantic, and he proved equally suited to all the different demands of British links.

It may well have come from the Irish blood in his veins, his parents having emigrated to South Africa before he was born. Certainly there was an 'Irish' quality to his swing. He hit everything with what is known as 'draw', manoeuvring the ball from right to left, even in his putts.

It may have been unconventional, but it was extraordinarily successful. Locke was also a scrambler of the highest class, a master of the wedge, which he helped to popularize in Britain, and a beautiful putter with a club that looked as if it had come out of the Ark.

Control of the ball, much more than power, was his strength while control of himself was not the least of his qualities. he never hurried, dismissed any disas-

trous hole instantly from his mind and while he was sometimes accused of being slow, he was certainly not by today's standards. He was also the most courteous of players and never other than immaculately dressed, best remembered for his plus fours and white cap.

Unlike most of the modern champions, Locke was not a great practiser. He preferred to play and did so happily with any club member who wanted a game. For 20 years he was unbeaten over 72 holes in South Africa and, but for the long periods he spent abroad, would have surely won his own national championship more than nine times.

Bobby Locke, a master of the controlled draw, and British Open champion four times.

131

Young Tom Morris wearing the Open championship belt he won outright with his third consecutive victory in 1870.

Tom Morris, Jr.
**Born St. Andrews 20 April 1851.
Died 1875.
Open champion 1868–69–70–72.**

Young Tom Morris, so described to distinguish him from his father, Old Tom, remains to this day the youngest man to have won the Open. He was 17 years and five months when in 1868 he took the first of four consecutive titles, which is similarly a record.

There was nevertheless a gap in the sequence. The hat-trick he completed at Prestwick in 1870 meant that the championship belt, which was then the prize, together with the then princely sum of £6, became his own property and consequently the Open was not played in 1871.

On its revival the following year Young Tom won again, but by then the Royal and Ancient and the Honourable Company of Edinburgh Golfers had joined forces with Prestwick in presenting the silver claret jug that now bears the names of more than 100 winners. These three clubs also shared the staging of the championship until, in 1894, it began to spread its wings by moving to England for the first time.

Young Tom therefore had a considerable influence on the ultimate history of the championship, the legend being enhanced by his death at the age of 24 of a 'broken heart', on Christmas Day, 1875. His young wife, whom he had adored, had died in childbirth together with their newly-born son, news of the tragedy reaching him as he tried to set sail from North Berwick, where he had been playing in a challenge match, so that he could be at her side.

Thus ended the domination of the championship by the Morrises. Old Tom had also won the title four times (1861–62–64–67) and thereby lies another piece of history unlikely to be repeated in that father and son were consecutive champions in 1867–68.

Perhaps the best example of Young Tom's ability is in his winning score at Prestwick in 1870. The course then consisted of 12 holes, which was played three times. He returned 149, which would be the equivalent today of rounds of 75, 74. With the gutty ball it was remarkable scoring – beyond even the capabilities of Harry Vardon, James Braid or J. T. Taylor when using similar equipment.

Young Tom was also a powerful hitter. In his last round in 1870 he had an eagle three at the first, which measured more than 500yd (455m). He was said to have broken many clubs even with his practice waggle and Old Tom admitted that though he could handle Allan Robertson, the greatest player in the country until his death in 1859, he could 'never cope wi' wee Tommy'.

His gravestone bears the inscription: 'Deeply regretted by numerous friends and all golfers, he thrice in succession won the championship belt and held it without rivalry and yet without envy'.

Byron Nelson

Born Fort Worth, Texas, 4 February 1912.
US Open champion 1939. Masters champion 1937–42. American PGA champion 1940–45. Ryder Cup 1937–47 (non-playing captain 1965).

Byron Nelson was a contemporary of Ben Hogan. Both were Texas born, learning their golf after first being caddies. Nelson reached his peak earlier, winning all his five major championships, beginning with the Masters in 1937 and ending with the PGA in 1945, before Hogan won his first in 1946.

Nelson's virtual retirement from competitive golf came just as Hogan was at last breaking through. Though a big man, he was not blessed with the most robust of health and as a haemophiliac was excused military service. But he could continue to play golf and no one has ever performed so consistently or maintained such a high level of play for so long.

In 1944 he won 13 out of 23 tournaments and the following year another 18 out of 31, including one astonishing sequence of 11 in a row, ten of them individual and the other in fourball play. He was also runner-up seven times, never out of the top ten and at one point played 19 consecutive rounds of under 70 and had a stroke average for the season of 68.33.

It was argued in some quarters that Nelson did not have the competition he would have had in peace time, many of the leading players being on active service. There were also concessions over preferred lies on fairways not always groomed to perfection and there was even some relaxation in the number of clubs players were allowed to carry.

Valid though this may be, it must also be said that, but for the war, Nelson would almost certainly have won more major championships. The US Open was suspended between 1942 and 1945, the Masters from 1943–45 and the British Open from 1940–45.

Consequently his British Open championship appearances were very limited. He was fifth behind Henry Cotton at Muirfield in 1937, having come over with the American Ryder Cup team, and he made only one more visit, in 1955, when he was long past his best. He was unable to do himself justice, though he did go on to win the French Open.

During that week in Paris, Nelson produced again the breathtaking iron play which was the hallmark of his game at its height. There was a machine-like quality about it, though such was his mastery of the long irons that he was never afraid to gamble. He was also an uncommonly fine driver of the ball.

After retirement, Nelson gained respect as one of the early television commentators, while his deep knowledge of the golf swing made him a coach with a considerable reputation. It was Nelson's guidance that helped to make Tom Watson.

Byron Nelson, who in 1945 won 11 consecutive American tournaments.

Jack Nicklaus

Born Columbus, Ohio, 21 January 1940.
Open champion 1966–70–78. US Open champion 1962–67–72–80. Masters champion 1963–65–66–72–75. American PGA champion 1963–71–73–75–80. US Amateur champion 1959–61. Ryder Cup 1969–71–73–75–77–81 (non-playing captain 1983). Walker Cup 1959–61.

In terms of the game's major championships, Jack Nicklaus is the greatest golfer of all time. Between 1962, the year he turned professional, and the fall of 1980, a span of 19 years. he won the Masters five times, the American PGA five times, the US Open four times and the British Open three times. That makes 17 – very nearly one a year.

Before that, in 1959 and 1961, he won the American Amateur twice, bringing his total of principal honours to 19, six more than the accumulation by Bobby Jones in the 1920s. It was a quite extraordinary run of success, though his consistency over an even longer spell was even more remarkable.

Between 1962 and the end of 1984 there were only two years (1969 and 1984) when Nicklaus did not win or come second in at least one of the major championships. In 92 consecutive appearances over 23 years he was, in addition to his 17 victories, runner-up 18 times, third nine times and in the top 10 on altogether 67 occasions. As an amateur he was also second behind Arnold Palmer in the US Open of 1960.

Only three other golfers have completed the 'set' of the British and US Opens, the Masters and the American PGA: Gene Sarazen, Ben Hogan and Gary Player, once each. Nicklaus has done it three times. In 1972 he was within two strokes of holding all four titles at the same time.

At the end of 1971 he had won the PGA for a second time and by June of 1972 he had added to it both the Masters and the US Open, one of five occasions when he took two of the four majors in the same year. But in the Open at Muirfield, despite a last round of 66, he lost by a stroke to Lee Trevino.

Even at the age of 15, when Nicklaus first appeared in the US Amateur, Bobby Jones later wrote of him: 'It was not difficult to see that a new talent of the first magnitude had arrived'. On a subsequent occasion, when Nicklaus won the 1965 Masters with a record total of 271, Jones remarked of the champion: 'He plays a game with which I am not familiar'.

Arnold Palmer, the great American hero, was at his peak when Nicklaus, in his rookie year of 1962, beat him in a play-off for the US Open at Oakmont. It was an upset not easily accepted by the golfing public for, with his crew-cut hair style and rather over-weight appearance, Nicklaus was regarded as a brash young collegiate.

In due course Nicklaus trimmed his body, grew his hair and, having seen himself once on television holing out with a cigarette in his mouth, never smoked on the course again. By the excellence of his power game, allied to the most delicate of touches on the greens, he has claimed 70 victories on the US tour with earnings in excess of $4.5 million, and gained world-wide popularity.

Jack Nicklaus, the most successful golfer in the history of the game.

Arnold Palmer in his halcyon days.

Arnold Palmer

**Born Latrobe. Pennsylvania,
10 September 1929.
Open champion 1961–62. US Open
champion 1960.
Masters champion 1958–60–62–64.
US Amateur champion 1954.
Ryder Cup 1961–63–65–67–71–73
(non-playing captain 1975).**

If any one man lit the fuse that set off the world-wide explosion in tournament golf, it was Arnold Palmer. He burst upon the scene in a manner and style that caught the public imagination as no one before him or, for that matter, since.

He was the embodiment of the 'nice guy next door' and yet with a presence about him that could leave the most senior captain of industry almost tongue-tied in his presence. The roar from a crowd that greets an Arnold Palmer birdie is still entirely special.

The Palmer image was created in 1960, when in the space of a few months he won both the Masters and US Open from positions that seemed hopeless. At Augusta he finished with three successive birdies to beat Ken Venturi by a stroke while at Cherry Hills, Colorado, he came from seven strokes behind going into the last round of the Open to win by two, playing the first nine holes in 30 on the way to a 65.

Such finishes became known as an 'Arnold Palmer charge' but though he was to win the Masters four times in seven years, his success at Cherry Hills was his only one in the US Open. Indeed Palmer was never quite the same again once he had lost a play-off to Jack Nicklaus at Oakmont in 1962.

It was still only Nicklaus' first year as a professional but it was clear that a formidable golfer had arrived. Palmer won only two more major championships after that, the British Open the same year and the Masters in 1964. Another play-off for the US Open was lost in 1963 – to Julius Boros – but it was Palmer's collapse against Billy Casper at Olympic, San Francisco, in 1966 that indicated his star was really in decline. Seven strokes ahead with nine to play, Palmer allowed himself to be caught and then lost the play-off the following day.

Palmer was largely responsible for reviving American interest in the British Open. He played first in the centenary Open at St. Andrews in 1960 where Kel Nagle, of Australia, beat him by a stroke, but came back the following year, winning at Royal Birkdale, again in 1962 and at Troon. Second, first and first again in three attempts was as unprecedented then as it is today.

Birkdale moreover was savaged by the sort of wild and wet days that can be a speciality of its Lancashire coast. Palmer's 73 in the second round, when the weather was at its worst, rated as one of his finest. He loved pitting his strength against the elements, for with his big hands and drive through the ball he was above all a golfer of aggression.

Palmer's respect for the traditions of the game and his sportsmanship became by-words wherever he travelled (often in his own aircraft) and under the guidance of Mark McCormack he not only became a multi-millionaire himself but paved the way for others to follow.

Gary Player

**Born Johannesburg, Transvaal,
1 November 1935.
Open champion 1959–68–74.
US Open champion 1965.
Masters champion 1961–74–78.
American PGA champion 1962–72.
South African Open champion
1956–60–65–66–67–68–69–72–75–76–77
–79–81.**

Gary Player's durability as a golfer of the highest class cannot be better demonstrated than by the fact that he won his first Open championship at the age of 23 in 1959, while at the age of 48 he was still good enough to be runner-up behind Lee Trevino in the 1984 American PGA championship.

The span of 15 years between his first Open victory and his third covered not only three different decades (1959–68–74) but is the longest since the distant days of J. H. Taylor, who put 19 years between his first and last victories, and Harry Vardon, who spanned 18 years. Yet Player has been defying the laws of probability all his life.

At 5ft 7in (1.7m) – which Player once jokingly remarked was Nicklaus' size at the age of 12 – he was far from blessed with the physique that breeds champions. He made up for it many times over with remarkable determination, being as fanatical over physical fitness and diet as he was ruthless over the hours he would spend on the practice ground.

Player was the first overseas golfer to win the Masters, in which he has now triumphed three times, while he is the only non-American to have completed the 'set' of the four major championships. For many years it was the South African's driving ambition to win the US Open a second time so that he could become the first foreigner to complete a second 'full house'.

Player nevertheless graduated to being regarded as one of the 'Big Three', along with Palmer and Nicklaus, and though he never had quite the same consistency as Nicklaus, he kept popping up again just when he seemed to have been forgotten.

A typical example of this came in the 1978 Masters when, 17 years after his first victory, he came from seven strokes behind to snatch the title with a last round of 64. It was reminiscent of one of his many sterling performances in the world match-play championship (which he won four times) at Wentworth as he fought back from seven down and 17 to play to defeat Tony Lema.

Player was also the first man to win the Open with the larger ball, made compulsory in 1974. In difficult, windy weather he was the only man to break 70 – which he did twice – all week, leading from start to finish.

From South Africa, where he owns a large farm, Player has undoubtedly flown more miles than any other golfer in search of conquests. These have come in abundance, not least in his seven Australian Open championships. Because of his nationality he has also been subjected to anti-apartheid demonstrations, once even having an armed guard on the course. In these difficult circumstances he proved himself as good an ambassador as he has been a golfer.

Gene Sarazen

Born Harrison, New York, 27 February 1902.
Open champion 1932. US Open champion 1922–32. Masters champion 1935. American PGA champion 1922–23–33.
Ryder Cup 1927–29–31–33–35–37.

In 1973 the Royal and Ancient invited all past Open champions to compete in that year's championship at Troon. One of the first to accept was Gene Sarazen, then 71. It marked the 50th anniversary of his first appearance in the Open when, on the same course and as the new star of American golf (he had won both the US Open and the PGA the year before), he failed to qualify.

Fifty years on he made much more of an impact. In the first round, partnered by two other past champions, Max Faulkner and Fred Daly, Sarazen holed in one at the Postage Stamp eighth. Briefly it even put him on the leader boards at one under par for the championship, while on the second day he was among the headlines again when he sank a bunker shot at the same hole for a two.

It was a most fitting finale for the cheerful, olive-skinned little man in plus fours whose career had spanned more than 50 years of championship golf. His contribution to it had also been considerable, not least because he was the first to win all four major professional titles.

Sarazen was in fact born Eugene Saraceni, changing his name because he thought it sounded as if he should be playing the violin. He would have become a carpenter but for poor health and he tried golf only as a means to getting fresh air. The game came so naturally to him that he won the US Open at Skokie, Illinois, at only his third attempt, aged 20.

The same year, 1922, he won the PGA and proved himself beyond all measure 12 months later when he retained this title, giving Walter Hagen his only defeat in the first of his five successive finals. These were also the years of Bobby Jones, and for a period Sarazen became lost in theory, abandoning his natural attacking instincts.

It took him until 1932 to win at last the British Open, his triumph at Prince's, which adjoins Royal St. George's, where he had been runner up to Hagen four years earlier, being in part due to his joining forces again with his faithful old caddie, Daniels.

At first Sarazen had declined the ageing man's services but he had second thoughts as he struggled in practice and immediately became a different man. He won comfortably, and promptly added his second US Open at Fresh Meadow, NY, when he played his last 28 holes in 100 strokes, including a final round of 66, which for many years stood as the lowest by a champion.

Sarazen, who invented the sand wedge, completed his 'set' of major titles by winning the Masters in 1935. An albatross two at the par five 15th, where he holed his second with a wooden club, enabled him to catch Craig Wood at the last gasp and he then won the play-off. That one stroke, Sarazen confessed, made him more money than any title.

Opposite: Gary Player, whose nine major championships include three British Opens in three different decades – 1959, 1968, 1974.

Below: Gene Sarazen at the British Open at Hoylake in 1924.

Sam Snead

**Born Hot Springs, Virginia,
27 May 1912.
Open champion 1946.
Masters champion 1949–52–54.
American PGA champion
1942–49–51.
Ryder Cup 1937–47–49–51–53–55–59
(non-playing captain 1969).**

Just as Arnold Palmer could never win the American PGA and Lee Trevino has never been able to win the Masters, so Sam Snead has always come unstuck in the United States Open. It is one of those inexplicable gaps in a golfing career that otherwise touched all the peaks.

He nevertheless came tantalizingly close, being runner-up to the US Open championship on four occasions. On one of those occasions, in 1947 at St. Louis, Snead tied with Lew Worsham but missed a putt of less than a yard on the 18th green in the play-off. It was an expensive error, but no more so than the eight he took at the final hole at

Philadelphia in 1939 when a five would have been sufficient, although he did not know it at the time. In those days the leaders did not go out last and there were fewer scoreboards.

Even so, Snead won 84 US tournaments in his career, which is substantially more than anyone else. His last came at the age of 52, while at 67 he even beat his age during one round of the Quad Cities Open. His lasting and lovely swing, born of an unusually supple body, enabled him to be a considerable force long after most players would have retired.

Snead was an exact contemporary of Ben Hogan and together they helped to build the Masters tournament into one of the most prestigious in the world, monopolizing the event between 1949 and 1954 when Snead won it three times and Hogan twice.

Because he alluded to Britain as 'camping out', Snead competed in the Open championship only three times, winning once, at St. Andrews in 1946. It was a last-minute decision, limited to a minimum of preparation but it was gained comfortably enough against a field still marshalling itself after the war, some indeed playing in their service uniforms.

All of Sam Snead's PGA championship competitions were in match-play, a type of game to which he was well suited and a reason why his Ryder Cup record was so good. In his seven singles, all over 36 holes, he was beaten only once, by Harry Weetman at Wentworth in 1953 when America tottered on the brink of defeat.

Sixteen years later, at Royal Birkdale in 1969, Snead was non-playing captain of another US side involved in a breathless finish as the two teams tied. He was said not to have been best pleased when Nicklaus generously conceded Tony Jacklin what seemed to be a missable putt for a half on the 18th green in the last game to finish, though it was a gesture that did Nicklaus a lot more good than harm.

Unlike Hogan, Snead even found a way of controlling the twitch, or yips, on the greens, taking a 'side-saddle' stance with the two hands far apart. It enabled him still to compete, for his long game was as pure as ever, and at the age of 62 he was still good enough to tie third in the PGA, three strokes behind the winner, Lee Trevino.

Sam Snead, whose enduring game is without comparison.

Peter Thomson, whose five British Open championships include a hat-trick between 1954–56.

Peter Thomson

Born Melbourne, Victoria, 23 August 1929.
Open champion 1954–55–56–58–65.
Australian Open champion 1951–67–72.

If Norman Von Nida could be looked upon as the grandfather of Australian golf, Peter Thomson could be regarded as its father. He was also a pioneer, journeying to the other side of the world to make a reputation that still stands.

Thomson is the only man this century to have won the British Open in three successive years (1954–56) and though Bobby Locke broke the sequence in 1957, Thomson was runner-up that year before he won for a fourth time in five years in 1958. The self-taught, quietly spoken and intelligent Australian had furthermore been runner-up to Ben Hogan in 1953, making him first or second for six consecutive years.

Admittedly it was all done at a time when the American armada had still to set sail in force across the Atlantic in the wake of Arnold Palmer in 1960. But there was no question as to Thomson's skill as a golfer and he had a splendidly simple method.

He never settled well in America (though he once came fourth in the US Open and fifth in the Masters) mainly perhaps because he was always a 'small ball man' who disliked the larger version then compulsory in the States. Even so he did win the 1956 Dallas Open, though the victory that gave him the greatest pleasure was his last in the British Open at Royal Birkdale in 1965 when he beat the likes of Tony Lema, the holder, Jack Nicklaus and Arnold Palmer. It put him alongside James Braid and J. H. Taylor as a five-time champion, a distinction since shared by Tom Watson.

In those days the last two rounds of the Open were played on the same day. It was Thomson's belief that to rest between those two rounds was dangerous. Consequently he would take a light lunch walking round until it was time to get to the first tee again.

Thomson represented Australia many times in the Canada Cup – later the World Cup – and partnered Kel Nagle in winning it twice. He won his own national championship three times and the New Zealand Open nine times.

As his playing career drew to a close, he turned his attention more to writing, broadcasting, golf course architecture, the development of the Far Eastern circuit and even politics until the increasing prize money on the American Seniors' tour drew him out of retirement.

Lee Trevino, the 'hustler' who became a champion.

Lee Trevino

Born Dallas, Texas, 1 December 1939.
Open champion 1971–72. US Open champion 1968–71. American PGA champion 1974–84. Ryder Cup 1969–71–73–75–79–81 (non-playing captain 1985).

There are, in a sense, three Lee Trevinos. The best known of course is the golfer; one who has triumphed twice each in the British Open, the US Open and the American PGA. Almost as well known is Trevino the clown; a bubbling, extrovert comedian who drops a succession of 'one liners' as rapidly and expertly as he hits stunning golf shots.

The third is the least known, though in fact it may well be 'the real' Lee Trevino. This is the intensely private man, who at the 1980 Open at Muirfield led an almost monk-like existence in the Greywalls Hotel, taking all his meals in his room, using none of the public rooms and avoiding even the main entrances as he went to and from his bedroom *via* a ground-floor French-window.

Such solitude is nothing unusual, for while Trevino is loved by millions, he is known only by a few. The banter, the fast tongue and the exuding warmth of the man are something he seems able to turn on with the flick of a switch. It is almost as if it is the generator of his golf.

Trevino learned his golf the hard way. A man of humble background, he was known as a 'hustler'; someone who would pit his skill against anyone in search of a dollar or a dime. It was a hard school but it taught him not only how to hit the ball but also how to play golf, which is much more important.

He was barely known when he won the US Open at Oak Hill in 1968. Yet he was the first and still only man to score in the 60s in every round – a distinction that he then astoundingly emulated in 1984 when, at the age of 44, he won the PGA for a second time at Shoal Creek.

Between those 16 years Trevino emerged for a time even as a threat to Jack Nicklaus, who was then at the height of his powers. Trevino beat him in a play-off for the 1971 US Open at Merion and within a few weeks had added to it the British Open, making him only the fourth man to have won these two titles in the same year, following Bobby Jones, Gene Sarazen and Ben Hogan.

Twelve months later, at Muirfield, Trevino retained the title, the 'hustler' in him coming to the surface as, in the course of four rounds, he holed three chips and a bunker shot. The most crucial was at the 71st hole for it gave him an unexpected lead and, at the same time, denied Tony Jacklin what seemed certain victory.

For a time Trevino's career was threatened by a chronic back condition, brought on when he was struck by lightning during the 1976 Western Open. Ultimately major surgery was required but though he had to cut down on practice, a second PGA victory in 1984 was testimony to his enduring ability.

Harry Vardon

Born Grouville, Jersey, 9 May 1870. Died 1937
Open champion 1896–98–99–1903–11–13. US Open champion 1900.

The name of Harry Vardon will always be linked with those of James Braid and J. H. Taylor. Together they formed what was known as the Great Triumvirate. It was hardly surprising: between 1894 and the outbreak of the first World War in 1914, a span of 21 years, they won the Open championship 16 times; Vardon recording a record six victories and Braid and Taylor five each.

There were also three occasions during those years when they filled the first three places and never a year went by when one of them was not in the first three. Only Peter Thomson and Tom Watson have since equalled the five victories of Braid and Taylor but Vardon's record still stands. It was the Triumvirate who first made the world aware of championship golf.

All three were born within 13 months of one another and although Taylor was the first English-born professional to win the Open, at Sandwich in 1894, it was Vardon who ultimately came to be looked upon as the greatest player. The 'Vardon grip', for instance, has gone into all the teaching manuals.

Vardon did not invent the grip, with the little finger of the right hand overlapping the first finger of the left, but helped to make it standard practice. There are still some players, notably Jack Nicklaus, who use an interlocking grip, with those two fingers entwined instead

Harry Vardon, Open champion six times, whose overlapping grip was written into all the teaching manuals.

of overlapping, and a few, like the late Dai Rees, who favour the double handed 'baseball' grip, but they are exceptions.

Vardon was also the first to bring grace and style to the golf swing. The more upright arc through which his club passed contrasted sharply with some of the flat-footed lunges of his predecessors and even contempories. By example he showed that rhythm and timing were more valuable than strength.

He nevertheless had the reputation of being a long hitter, though the clubs he used were light in weight and never more than ten in number. Though half of his six Opens were won with the rubber-cored ball, it was with the gutty that he was said to be at his best.

Vardon was the first visitor from abroad to win a US Open, at Chicago in 1900, and he also lost in a three-way play-off at The Country Club, Brookline, 13 years later to an unknown amateur, Francis Ouimet, whose victory lit the fuse to the American upsurge in the game.

Tom Watson

Born Kansas City, Missouri, 4 September 1949.
Open champion 1975–77–80–82–83.
US Open champion 1982. Masters champion 1977–81.
Ryder Cup 1977–81–83.

There have not been many disappointments in the career of Tom Watson. But if he had the opportunity to turn back the clock he would undoubtedly do it to the time when he stood on the 17th fairway in the final round of the 1984 Open at St. Andrews.

Tied at that point with Severiano Ballesteros, Watson was to finish 5,4, against the Spaniard's 4,3, and a dream was shattered. To have equalled Harry Vardon's record of six Open titles would have been one thing; to have done it at the home of golf would, as Americans are inclined to put it, have been 'something else'.

It would also have been a hat-trick of championships for Watson had won both

at Royal Troon in 1982 and at Royal Birkdale in 1983. As it is, his five victories in the space of ten years came in an unprecedented short time, quickly putting him alongside James Braid, J. H. Taylor and Peter Thomson.

If one year more than any other was the making of Tom Watson, it was 1977 when he twice confronted Jack Nicklaus 'eyeball to eyeball' and did not flinch. At Augusta in the Masters, Nicklaus, three strokes behind, fired a typical last round of 66; but Watson had a 67 and won by two.

Then at Turnberry the same year in the Open they matched one another shot for shot for three days with 68–70–65 before Watson got home by a finger-nail in the final round with another 65 to Nicklaus' 66. It was the most riveting struggle between two men at the peak of their form that championship golf has probably ever known; perfectly climaxed when first Nicklaus holed for a birdie on the last green and then Watson followed him for another and the title.

For all that – and despite his being leading money winner in the States for four successive years beginning in 1977 – Watson still had his critics. After early failures in the US Open he was labelled a 'choker'. When he disproved that, his driving was called to question, particularly on the tight US Open courses.

When at last he won the US Open, at Pebble Beach in 1982, it was in the most dramatic fashion and once again Nicklaus was his victim. Two birdies by Watson at the last two holes were all that separated them but it was his chip-in for a two at the 17th, when it looked odds on his taking four, that was crucial.

Just as Nicklaus was regarded suspiciously, even grudgingly, when first he was challenging the supremacy of Arnold Palmer, so was Watson when he was hunting and then beating Nicklaus. But by the crispness of his play, the excellence of his short game (particularly his putting) and, not least, his sincerity as a man, he has gained a respect equal to that of any of the great champions.

Tom Watson, who has always born those twin imposters, triumph and disaster, just the same.

Joyce Wethered with the British women's championship trophy she won at Troon in 1925.

Joyce Wethered

Born Witley, Surrey, 17 November 1901.
British Women's champion 1922–24–25–29. English Women's champion 1920–21–22–23–24. Curtis Cup 1932.

Whenever a golfer holes a putt against a background of some sudden and unlikely noise or disturbance, someone is almost certain to utter aloud or under their breath: 'What train?' Such a remark would leave a non-golfer entirely baffled.

It is nevertheless a legendary anecdote attributed to Joyce Wethered, now Lady

Heathcoat-Amory, when winning an English championship at Sheringham, Norfolk. She happened to hole an important putt just as a local train rumbled past and when asked why it had not disturbed her, she replied in all innocence: 'What train?'

It gives an insight into the powers of concentration of someone whom Bobby Jones, never one inclined to overstatement, once described as the finest golfer, man or woman, he had ever seen.

Miss Wethered, as she then was, brought a grace and beauty to the golf swing that some say has never been matched. She once said that when playing at her best she had the feeling that at the top of the backswing nothing on earth could dislodge her from her right foot while at the finish of the follow-through, nothing could equally shift her from her left. She had, in other words, supreme balance.

Rhythm, timing, speed of hand, all combined to make her a longer hitter than her contemporaries while she also had the temperament that is found only in champions, the span of her career at the top lasting nine years.

Her arrival on the scene at the age of 19 had immediate impact for, not least to her own surprise, she won the English Championship, defeating the then Queen of women's golf, 'Cecil' Leitch, in the final. It was the first of several confrontations.

They met again the following year in the final of the British championship as well as in the final of the French, Miss Leitch winning each time. However Miss Wethered levelled the score again in 1922 as she won her first British title, and then they met yet again, in the 1925 final of the British.

Again it was Miss Wethered who prevailed in a marvellous match that went to the 37th, whereupon she retired for three years before being lured back by the prospect of the championship being played at St. Andrews. Rising typically to the occasion she defeated Glenna Collett, an outstanding American player, by three and one having at one point been five down.

Altogether she won four of the six British championships she entered, had an unbeaten run of 33 matches in taking the English title for five successive years and then, in 'retirement', enjoyed eight victories in the Worplesdon foursomes with seven different male partners.

Mildred (Babe) Zaharias

Born Port Arthur, Texas, 26 June 1914. Died 1956.
US Women's Open Champion 1948–50–54. US Women's Amateur Champion 1946. British Women's Amateur Champion 1947.

'Babe' Zaharias was not only one of the greatest women golfers the world has known; she was also the most gifted of athletes, having a natural aptitude for all games. Indeed she was a sporting phenomenon before she ever took a golf club in her hands – and when, incidentally, she is reputed to have knocked the ball more than 200yd (182m) with her first hit.

Born Mildred Didrikson, she became known as 'The Babe' when as a 17-year-old in the American Track and Field championships which preceded the 1932 Olympic Games she won six of the seven events for which she entered. In the Olympics themselves she was limited to only three – the hurdles, javelin and high jump – and won them all. However, her gold medal in the high jump was later disallowed because of her, then illegal, method of going over the bar head first.

Zaharias also reached All-America status as a basketball player, played competitive baseball and softball, showed distinct promise as a tennis player and was an expert diver, roller-skater and bowler. Golf came to her just as easily when she took it up; blessed with unusual power for a woman – her game resembling more that of a man –

she quickly reached the highest standards.

She was nevertheless always a slightly controversial figure and having won the Texas Open in 1935, was declared a professional. After marrying an all-in wrestler in 1938, she applied for reinstatement as an amateur but it took five years to materialize.

Zaharias promptly ran amok, winning in 1946 and 1947 no less than 17 events in a row. They included the US Amateur and the British Women's title at Gullane, Scotland, where she was ordered back into the clubhouse to change, having first appeared in a kilt worn over a pair of slacks.

She also scorned tradition by painting her fingernails and wearing make-up on the course. However it was still her golf that made the biggest impact, Enid Wilson observing in her *Gallery of Women Golfers* that Zaharias 'moved like a ballerina, as though she did not have a bone in her body'.

When 'The Babe' turned professional a second time – now of her own accord – she promptly won her first US Open at Atlantic City in 1948 and then regained the title two years later at Rolling Hills. She was a founder member of the LPGA tour and won 31 tournaments.

What really plucked at the heartstrings of everybody however was her fight against cancer. Zaharias underwent surgery in 1953 and a year later came back to win her third US Open title by a record 12 strokes. In fact she won five tournaments that year and another two in 1955. But she lost her battle against the disease which finally claimed her in 1956.

'Babe' Zaharias, perhaps the greatest all-round woman athlete of all.

4 THE GREAT COURSES

The peace and tranquillity of Augusta National's 12th hole, which comes at the apex of Amen Corner.

Augusta National, Georgia, USA.

No tournament is more eagerly awaited each year than the Masters at Augusta National. Falling as it does in April, it is the launching pad of a new season – a sort of grand reunion as golfers from all parts of the globe come together on the lawns fronting the discreetly elegant green and white clubhouse.

In a sense this was how Bobby Jones envisaged it when he and the distinguished Scottish architect, Dr. Alister Mackenzie, first saw the possibilities of building a course on land that used to be a nursery and then set about designing it.

The club, which has a very small and exclusive membership, was founded in 1931. The first Masters was played in 1934, 'just among a few friends' of Jones; but what put both the tournament and Augusta on the map was the 1935 Masters when Gene Sarazen had an albatross two at the 15th in the final round to catch Craig Wood before beating him in the play-off.

If two holes are talked about more than any other, they are the 13th and 15th, both par fives but reachable in two for the longer hitters provided they have got both the skill and the nerve. Immediately in front of the 13th green there is a twisting brook and in front of the domed 15th green a pond, usually dyed blue for the occasion.

These two holes are invariably critical on the last afternoon of the Masters, coming as they do at the climax to the tournament. But Augusta, they say, does not really 'begin' until the second nine

holes, treacherous particularly at the 11th, 12th and 13th with water close to each green and known as Amen Corner.

It is not, for all that, a particularly difficult course. The concept from the beginning was to make it eminently playable for the average mortal, but at the same time to test the expert searching for a low score. The fairways are consequently wide and there is no rough, only trees.

But the greens are big, fiercely undulating and extremely fast. The art lies not in getting the ball on the green but in finding the right place close enough to the hole for the chance of a birdie putt. No course is more immaculately tended nor, when the shrubs are ablaze with colour, more beautiful.

THE CARD

Hole		Yards	Par	Hole		Yards	Par
1	White Pine	400	4	10	Camelia	485	4
2	Woodbine	555	5	11	Dogwood	445	4
3	Flowering Peach	360	4	12	Golden Bell	155	3
4	Palm	220	3	13	Azalea	485	5
5	Magnolia	450	4	14	Chinese Fir	420	4
6	Juniper	190	3	15	Fire Thorn	520	5
7	Pampas	365	4	16	Red Bud	190	3
8	Yellow Jasmine	530	5	17	Nandina	400	4
9	Caroline Cherry	440	4	18	Holly	420	4
		3,510	36			3,520	36

Total 7,030yd (6,397m) Par 72.

Ballybunion, County Kerry, Eire.

A golfer's education is incomplete unless he has played Ballybunion. It takes a good day's march to get there however, perched as it is on the western cliffs of Ireland and overlooking the Atlantic with America the next stop, some 3,000 miles (4,830km) away.

But for its remoteness, Ballybunion would undoubtedly have played a more prominent part in the development of both Irish and British championship golf. Yet it is also this very seclusion, in a part of the world where time stands still, that provides its whole attraction.

No other course in the British Isles has such vast sandhills, fairways winding in between them, greens perched on ledges and a succession of views that repeatedly take the breath away. Herbert Warren Wind, the doyen of American golf writers, once described it as 'nothing less than the finest seaside course I have ever seen'.

It is a sentiment shared by Tom Watson, who was introduced to Ballybunion by Sandy Tatum, then President of the USGA, on his way to play in the Open one year. So captivated was Watson that he has been back more than once, able to touch down at Shannon airport, which is not too far away.

The building of a new clubhouse at a different part of the course has improved appearances for hitherto it meant that the 17th and 18th holes were both par fives. Now they play as the fourth and fifth and it is after that that all the glories of Ballybunion unfold.

Unusually there are not only successive par fives but successive par threes as well (the 15th and 16th) but these are imbalances that one is willing to forgive for the sheer pleasure of meeting the challenge of the place. There is a special thrill about hitting a good shot at Ballybunion.

Yet the education is never complete until one has also experienced one of those wild and windy days when the sea and sky somehow become one and the sudden squalls of rain sting the face pink. To play golf then is as invigorating as it is mad.

And there is always, at the end of it, the unique experience of Irish hospitality. That can be as timeless as the course itself.

Carnoustie, Tayside, Scotland.

In the days when it was fashionable to give golf holes names, the tenth at Carnoustie was christened South America after one of the locals who had decided to emigrate but never got any further. He had imbibed rather too well at his farewell party!

Of some 300 young men of Carnoustie who have become professional golfers, two who did emigrate, Willie and Alex Smith, went on to become United States Open champions. The compliment has been returned most notably by Ben Hogan in 1953 and Tom Watson in 1975.

It was at Carnoustie that Hogan won his only British Open – in a year during which he had also taken the Masters and US Open – and Watson won the first of five Open titles in the astonishingly short span of nine years. Sadly that was the last time the championship was staged on these East of Scotland links close to the North Sea.

By common agreement, there is no more demanding test of links golf in the British Isles, with scarcely a weak hole anywhere, splendid variation and a finish of classic proportions. In the modern arena of championship golf, however, these are ancillary considerations.

Space for tented villages, extensive car parking and hotel accommodation are now as important as the course itself, though it is inconceivable that Carnoustie's disappearance will be a permanent one. It is simply too good, although it brought from Hogan an almost clinical dissection with rounds ever lower than the last – 73, 71, 70, 68.

Henry Cotton was also at his most ruthless here in 1937, destroying a field that included the whole of the visiting American Ryder Cup team, while Gary Player enjoyed one of his finest hours in

THE CARD

Hole	Yard	Par	Hole	Yards	Par
1	377	4	10	356	4
2	434	4	11	443	4
3	217	3	12	185	3
4	504	5	13	485	5
5	508	5	14	136	3
6	364	4	15	228	3
7	417	4	16	483	5
8	151	3	17	379	4
9	455	4	18	381	4
	3,427	36		3,076	35

Total 6,503yd (5,918m) Par 71

Left: Ballybunion's 17th hole, the Atlantic in the background.

Below: Carnoustie's 18th green with the thin line of the Barry Burn crossing the fairway.

1968 when he held off a late and spirited assault from Jack Nicklaus.

Player's eagle three at the 14th, where he hit a spoon shot to within a yard of the hole, was all-important; as was Watson's birdie three at the 18th to earn a tie with Jack Newton and then a four at the same hole in the play-off the following day for victory. It turned his whole career.

The last hole had then been reduced to a par four, bringing the famous Barry Burn in front of the green more into play; a vast, coiling snake it is everywhere over Carnoustie's two finishing holes.

THE CARD

Hole		Yards	Par	Hole		Yards	Par
1	Cup	406	4	10	South America	453	4
2	Gulley	464	4	11	Dyke	372	4
3	Jockie's Burn	384	4	12	Southward Ho!	478	5
4	Hillocks	379	4	13	Whin's	166	3
5	Brae	397	4	14	Spectacles	488	5
6	Long	524	5	15	Luckyslap	461	4
7	Plantation	397	4	16	Barry Burn	235	3
8	Short	174	3	17	Island	454	4
9	Railway	421	4	18	Home	448	4
		3,546	36			3,555	36

Total: 7,101yd (6,462m) Par 72

Cypress Point, California, USA.

If, for some reason, one were to be confined to playing only one golf course for the remainder of one's life, it is more than likely that the choice would be Cypress Point on the spectacular and beautiful Monterey Peninsula. It bears the hand of Alister Mackenzie, which was the principal reason why Bobby Jones subsequently invited him to help in the design of Augusta National.

There may not be another golf course in the world with such infinite variety: from seaside to cliff top, from wooded hillside to inland and though not, at 6,464yd (5,882m) quite of championship length, it is not everybody who would want to commit himself to a longer slog for the rest of his days.

The small and privileged membership also ensures that the course is seldom crowded, though it does each year open its doors to the popular Bing Crosby pro-am tournament, which is played concurrently on two other courses, at Pebble Beach and Spyglass Hill.

The Walker Cup match staged here in 1981 also gave the British and their supporters the rare opportunity to sample for themselves a course which possesses what is almost certainly the most photographed hole in the world.

The 16th, a short hole of 233yd (212m) is played over two inlets of rugged coastline with the surging Pacific beating on the rocks far below. It provides therefore a daunting carry from the tee beyond the far cliff and hardly anyone can resist the temptation to 'have a go' at least once. They will surely tell their grandchildren about it if they make it, but anyone with the rights to re-sell all the golf balls that have plunged into the surf below would be a millionaire.

The alternative route, via a medium iron shot to a fairway on the left of the

two inlets, leaves the chances of a par three depending on a single putt, but nevertheless there are even professionals who always play the hole that way.

Together with the 15th, a much shorter but in many ways similar hole, and 17th, where the drive must again be bravely aimed across the ocean to an angled fairway, this is a sequence of holes without equal. Just the smallest slip can, in a flash, ruin the best of cards, but nothing is more certain than that, once accomplished, the urge to repeat the experience will be irresistible.

	THE CARD				
Hole	Yard	Par	Hole	Yards	Par
1	420	4	10	477	5
2	544	5	11	433	4
3	161	3	12	411	4
4	384	4	13	361	4
5	490	5	14	387	4
6	521	5	15	139	3
7	160	3	16	233	3
8	338	4	17	375	4
9	291	4	18	339	4
	3,309	37		3,155	35

Total: 6,464yd (5,882m) Par 72

El Saler, Valencia, Spain.

When the West German, Bernhard Langer, assured himself of being the leading money-winner of 1984 in Europe, he did so by taking the Spanish Open at El Saler with a final round of 62. It was an astounding exhibition of golf on the best course in Spain.

It was designed by Spain's best known architect, Javier Arana, who was also responsible for El Prat, in Barcelona, and Club de Campo, in Madrid, among others. At more than 7,000yd (6,370m), El Saler is longer than either of the others though it is not so much this as its infinite variety that appeals.

Among the features of Spanish courses are the many umbrella pines which border the fairways. In isolated cases these can even be found on the fairways, and they provide obstructions in defence of a green for a shot from the wrong angle. However, El Saler offers much more than that.

Hard on the shores of the Mediterranean, a 30-minute drive south of

El Saler, perhaps the finest course designed by the Spanish architect, Javier Arana.

Valencia, it also provides splendid links golf that stirs distinct memories of Portmarnock, in Ireland. Big, sloping greens nestle in the sandhills and the land gently rises and falls like the swell on the adjacent sea.

A feature, too, is the generous width to the fairways, which call for a driver rather than a defensive long iron from the tee, while the bunkers are magnificently big and deep, appearing natural amid the contours of the terrain. El Saler looks as if it was always meant to be a golf course.

The par fives are also very much par fives, since all of them are well in excess of 500yd (455m) only the third having a weakness since it was discovered that there is a shorter, though perhaps more dangerous, route via the second fairway. Even the short holes are long, three of the four being 190yd (173m) and more.

Unusually, it is a State-managed course, having been commissioned by the Ministry of Information and Tourism to attract visitors from overseas, and has one of a chain of hotels overlooking both the course and the sea. But although it is a public course, it is seldom, if ever, as busy as those along the Costa del Sol.

THE CARD

Hole	Yard	Par	Hole	Yards	Par
1	440	4	10	410	4
2	405	4	11	565	5
3	530	5	12	205	3
4	190	3	13	355	4
5	520	5	14	420	4
6	450	4	15	565	5
7	370	4	16	430	4
8	370	4	17	215	3
9	160	3	18	370	4
	3,435	36		3,635	36

Total: 7,070yd (6,434m) Par 72.

Durban Country Club, Natal, South Africa.

It cannot be often that two brothers are 'in at the death' of a national championship but it was at Durban Country Club in 1928 that Jack Brews gained a remarkable victory over his brother, Sid, in the South African Open.

Sid, the holder, was in the clubhouse with a 72-hole score of 298 when Jack came to the last needing a birdie three to tie. He went one better than that, driving the green 276yd (251m) away and then holing the putt for an eagle two and victory by a stroke. It was his fourth and last title; Sid, who had followed his brother in emigrating to South Africa, bettering him by two with six championships.

Seldom are tournaments, let alone championships, won with an eagle at the last hole and the fact that the 18th at Durban Country Club, which is not far from the shore of the Indian Ocean, can be driven could be regarded as a weakness. In fact it is a much more challenging hole than that, the fairway being hog's back in shape, with sharp drops both right and left.

Both the start and finish are very reminiscent of a British duneland course with big, undulating fairways that are particularly difficult to find when the wind off the ocean is sending great breakers crashing down on the shore. As rapidly the course can change, almost as if one had suddenly sailed into a calm.

Some seven or eight holes around the turn are very much on the flat, though not the short 12th, which requires a seven or eight iron shot to a bowler-hatted green. It once took the late Duke of Windsor, a keen golfer, 17 strokes to hole out as he played a form of 'ping pong' from one side to the other.

Yet the club only came into being when its neighbour, Royal Durban, which is now in the middle of the city racecourse, flooded so badly in the 1919 South African Open that the winner took 320 strokes. The new course was built to ensure Durban's continuing place on the golfing roster.

There have been a number of changes from the original design but it has continued to play a central part in the history of South African golf. It was here that Gary Player won the first of his many open championships, in 1956, and here as well that Sewsunker 'Papwa' Sewgolum, a black player with the unusual grip of left hand below right, won the Natal Open in 1962 and 1965.

THE CARD					
Hole	Yard	Par	Hole	Yards	Par
1	390	4	10	550	5
2	182	3	11	456	4
3	506	5	12	147	3
4	172	3	13	337	4
5	459	4	14	514	5
6	349	4	15	166	3
7	383	4	16	375	4
8	498	5	17	392	4
9	424	4	18	276	4
	3,363	36		3,213	36
Total: 6,576yd (5,984m) Par 72					

Merion, Philadelphia, USA.

Merion has the distinction of having been the scene of the end and the beginning of two of the most successful careers in the history of golf. It was here in 1930 that Bobby Jones beat Eugene Homans in the final of the American Amateur championship by eight and seven to complete what he liked to call the 'Impregnable Quadrilateral' of the first Grand Slam, winning both the Open and Amateur championships of Britain and the United States in the same year. He thereupon retired.

It was also at Merion, in 1960, that Jack Nicklaus, a raw and muscular 20-year-old, assisted the USA to the first of its many victories in the world amateur team championship for the Eisenhower Trophy with rounds of 66, 67, 68, 68: scarcely believable scoring by a young amateur on what was ackowledged as one of the severest tests of golf in the country.

What separates Merion from the vast majority of other championship courses the world over is its length. At 6,544yd (5,955m) it is much shorter than would normally be acceptable. Yet it has now staged four US Opens and been a regular host to all manner of other events under the control of the USGA.

In these days of the power game, when length seems to be the only criteria as stronger and stronger players hit better and better golf balls further and further with ever-improving equipment, Merion is testimony to the declining belief that there is more to golf than sheer

Among the features at Merion are the wild clumps of grass in the bunkers and the oval wicker baskets instead of flags.

strength. No less than six of its par fours are of less than 400yd (364m).

It has several other distinguishing features, notable among them a profusion of bunkers, known as 'the white faces of Merion', with tall clumps of spiky grass protruding from their midst which make straightforward recovery shots extremely difficult, if not impossible. Another is the oval wicker baskets which top the flagsticks.

Yet it is the greens themselves which are the best defence of the course. They are so fiercely quick that Walter Hagen once putted out of bounds at the 12th, his ball finishing up on Ardmore Avenue, a thoroughfare dividing seven holes (the first and the last six) from the rest. There are few more testing finishes than the last five holes.

Australian David Graham completed them in two under par for a final round of 67 to win the 1981 US Open with as flawless an exhibition of stroke-making as had been seen by a champion for many years; certainly in the class of Ben Hogan on the same course 31 years earlier.

THE CARD

Hole	Yard	Par	Hole	Yards	Par
1	355	4	10	312	4
2	535	5	11	370	4
3	183	3	12	405	4
4	600	5	13	129	3
5	426	4	14	414	4
6	420	4	15	378	4
7	350	4	16	430	4
8	360	4	17	224	3
9	195	3	18	458	4
	3,424	36		3,120	34

Total: 6,544yd (5,955m) Par 70

Muirfield, East Lothian, Scotland.

Muirfield, the home of the Honourable Company of Edinburgh Golfers, is accepted as being the oldest club in the world. Its records date back to 1744 and it was also responsible for drawing up the original rules of golf. They were 13 in number and, unlike the modern set, a masterpiece of brevity.

Together with the Royal and Ancient, which was founded 10 years later in 1754, the Honourable Company also linked with Prestwick in the organization of the Open championship on its revival in 1872, the three clubs taking it in turns to play host until 1894 when, for the first time, the championship was played in England, at Royal St. George's, Sandwich.

By then Muirfield had found its third and final home, high on the shore of the Firth of Forth, looking north across the estuary to the Kingdom of Fife. Hitherto the club had had headquarters at Leith and then Musselburgh, which staged six Opens before the move to Muirfield in 1891.

Other than St. Andrews itself, Muirfield is the oldest venue on the Open Championship roster and is considered by many also to be the best and fairest, possibly because the bounce of the ball is more predictable than on many seaside links. The fairways are flatter on land sloping gently towards the shore and, apart from the 11th, where the drive is blind over a ridge in the sand dunes, all the hazards are in full view from the tee.

These take the shape of some of the most classic and deepest bunkers in

Britain, gathering shots that on other courses might just escape. There is also a continual shift in direction as the course goes clockwise for nine holes and then, within that outer rim, anti-clockwise for the inward half. It is therefore the ideal watching course with any number of short cuts and the extremities never more than two holes from the clubhouse.

The rough can be very severe, never more so than in 1966 when Jack Nicklaus won the first of his three Opens, frequently driving with a one iron to avoid 'the hay'. In 1948 Henry Cotton was equally successful in keeping out of trouble, missing only four fairways from the tee in 72 holes as he won the title for the third time.

Ryder, Walker and Curtis Cups have all been held at Muirfield, Britain's ladies gaining there one of only two victories against the USA, in 1952. Yet for all its popularity as a venue for the big occasion, Muirfield is a very private club, has no professional's shop and plays nearly all its competitions by foursomes.

THE CARD					
Hole	Yard	Par	Hole	Yards	Par
1	449	4	10	475	4
2	349	4	11	386	4
3	379	4	12	381	4
4	181	3	13	153	3
5	558	5	14	447	4
6	471	4	15	396	4
7	185	3	18	188	3
8	444	4	17	542	5
9	495	5	18	447	4
	3,511	36		3,415	35

Total: 6,926yd (6,303m) Par 71

The 18th green at Muirfield, home of the Honourable Company of Edinburgh Golfers.

Muirfield Village, Dublin, Ohio, USA.

Jack Nicklaus' first visit to Britain was as a member of the 1959 US Walker Cup team. The match was played at Muirfield in Scotland. Seven years later he returned to win the Open for the first time and complete his 'set' of the world's four major titles. When, therefore, Nicklaus designed his first golf course in the rolling, wooded countryside in his home state of Ohio, it was hardly surprising that the strong nostalgic streak running through his veins should persuade him to name it Muirfield Village; the club crest also carries the outline of the Open Championship trophy, encircled by laurel leaves.

Typically of Nicklaus, there was a total attention to detail in designing his course. It has always been his belief that no golfer likes driving uphill. Consequently, with a seemingly bottomless purse to accommodate his every whim,

he made sure that every tee offered either a downhill shot or, at least, one along the flat, even if it meant bulldozing the land.

Once he changed his mind about the stream running in front of the 11th green, a long par five, and instructed that it be turned into a lake. Then he did not like that, either, and turned it back into a stream. As with Augusta, which almost annually sees some subtle change, Nicklaus is repeatedly making adjustments to the course in search of perfection.

Muirfield Village was one of the first courses to be built very much with the spectator in mind. On some holes more than 20,000 people have an unobstructed view and within two years of the course being opened in 1974 it staged the first of the now annual Memorial tournaments which Nicklaus himself has won twice, in 1977 and 1984.

It is doubtful whether any course in the world is better prepared and few are better balanced. The number of dog-leg holes to the right equal those to the left and all the time there is the gurgling brook running across or parallel to many of the fairways. At the fifth, it travels up the spine, so that there is no alternative but to go left or right.

A circular practice ground, giving the golfer the choice of wind direction, is not the least of the many offerings while the Memorial tournament itself, which honours each year some golfing statesman, is Nicklaus' way of paying tribute to the champions who inspired his own career.

	THE CARD				
Hole	Yard	Par	Hole	Yards	Par
1	446	4	10	441	4
2	452	4	11	538	5
3	392	4	12	158	3
4	214	3	13	442	4
5	531	5	14	363	4
6	430	4	15	490	5
7	549	5	16	204	3
8	174	3	17	430	4
9	410	4	18	437	4
	3,598	36		3,503	36
		Total: 7,101yd (6,462m) Par 72			

Right: Muirfield Village, 'the course that Jack built'. The 14th hole.

Opposite: An example of the terrors of Pine Valley. The 185-yd (168m) 14th.

Pine Valley, Philadelphia, USA.

Pine Valley has been described as both a '184-acre bunker' and 'the most difficult inland course in the world'. Bearing that in mind, the story of Woody Platt, a local amateur who once played the first four holes in six under par, has gone down as the most famous of all its tales.

Platt started with a birdie three and then holed his approach shot for an eagle two at the second which, to a partially blind green beyond a mass of sand and scrub, is regarded as one of Pine Valley's toughest holes. The third is a par three, where he holed his tee shot.

That made him five under par and when he sank his putt for a birdie at the fourth to go six under, he was in such a state of excitement that he felt the need to calm his nerves with a glass of something in the clubhouse, which he had to pass on his way to the fifth tee. But one glass became two, then three, and one way and another Woody never did get around to playing the remaining 14 holes.

He was probably wise, for it is highly likely that Pine Valley would have extracted full revenge within a hole or two. Hitting a ball from and to a series of islands across unattended sandy wastes dotted with clumps of grass and bush, poses problems even for the best. The members have long since taken bets that anyone playing the course for the first time will not break 80 and, while there have been exceptions (like Arnold Palmer, who had a 68), they invariably collect the money.

Pine Valley was the creation of a Philadelphia hotelier, George Crump. He saw the possibilities amid a forest of pine, but more than 20,000 trees needed to be uprooted and altogether it took seven years for the course to be completed. Sadly Crump never saw the finished article. He died with the last few holes still under construction but, with the help of the British architect, H. S. Colt, he left behind a masterpiece.

Many of the holes are considered to be classics and neither of the two par fives, one 585yd (532m) and the other 603yd (549m) have ever been reached in two strokes. But such is the terrain that it has not been possible to stage there a professional tournament because it is a near-hopeless spectator course. It did however host both the 1936 and 1985 Walker Cup matches.

THE CARD					
Hole	Yard	Par	Hole	Yards	Par
1	427	4	10	145	3
2	367	4	11	399	4
3	185	3	12	382	4
4	461	4	13	446	4
5	226	3	14	185	3
6	391	4	15	603	5
7	585	5	16	436	4
8	327	4	17	344	4
9	432	4	18	424	4
	3,401	35		3,364	35

Total 6,765yd (6,156m) Par 70.

The ninth green at Portmarnock, with Howth Hill in the background.

Portmarnock, Dublin, Eire.

There was a time when the only way to reach Portmarnock was either by boat or, at low tide, horse-drawn cart across the mud flats. Now there is narrow track, a mile in length, leading from the main road between Sutton and Malahide. On the days of a big tournament, like the Irish Open, it is packed nose to tail with cars, but in Ireland time waits for every man.

There has been talk of constructing a bridge across the small estuary but somehow that would disturb the peace and naturalness of what many consider to be Ireland's finest test of golf; although even its admirers would agree that it is a 'close run thing' when compared to Royal County Down, Ballybunion and Royal Portrush.

Portmarnock is certainly the longest of the four and very much a links, set as it is on a peninsula between the inland tidal bay and, on its eastern flank, the Irish Sea, from which rise two distant rocky islands, one known as Ireland's Eye and the other Lambay. Overlooked by Howth Hill to the south and a fine beach running north, it can be a heavenly place on the right day.

On others it can be fiercely testing as a prevailing south-westerly blows in from the direction of the fair city of Dublin, making some already long holes even longer. An easterly, too, causes problems, particularly at the 15th, a fine and longish 'short' hole running parallel to the beach, over which the ball must sometimes be aimed.

The three short holes are among the particular enchantments of Portmarnock: and nicely varied, with the 12th a little gem, a cunning green sitting among the sand dunes. Equally there are only three par fives and the high proportion of par fours and make it a hard course on which to score well.

Unusually for a links, the ninth comes back to the red-roofed clubhouse, the course describing a vague figure of eight with consequent repeated change of direction. There are also few blind shots, though the land is far from flat as the deep bunkers mould themselves into its many contours.

The Irish are as knowledgeable as they are fanatic about their golf and nothing has given them greater pleasure than Max McCready's victory in the British Amateur here in 1949; unless it was Chirsty O'Connor's in the 1959 Dunlop Masters when a final round of 66 stole the title from another of Ireland's favourite sons, the amateur Joe Carr.

THE CARD					
Hole	Yard	Par	Hole	Yards	Par
1	388	4	10	380	4
2	368	4	11	445	4
3	388	4	12	144	3
4	460	4	13	565	5
5	407	4	14	385	4
6	586	5	15	192	3
7	180	3	16	527	5
8	370	4	17	466	4
9	444	4	18	408	4
	3,591	36		3,512	36

Total: 7,103yd (6,464m) Par 72

Pebble Beach, California USA.

Whenever Pebble Beach crops up in conversation, minds go back to the 1982 United States Open and that dramatic finish as Tom Watson stole the title from his great rival Jack Nicklaus, for whom a record five victories seemed not so much to beckon as to be within his very grasp.

Nicklaus had already finished when Watson came to the 17th needing two pars to tie. When he missed the green on the left, leaving him a most difficult chip to save par, his chances were slim indeed. Instead Watson, with that masterful touch of his around the greens, holed it

for a two and then made totally sure of his first US Open with another birdie, this time a four, at the last.

Strangely for an American course of such outstanding fame and reputation, this was only the second time that the championship had been held at Pebble Beach. On the previous occasion, in 1972, Nicklaus had been the winner and, by a coincidence, it was his two at the 17th in the final round that finally shut the door on his pursuers, among them Arnold Palmer.

This, in a sense, completed a Nicklaus 'double' for in 1961 it was also at Pebble Beach that he collected his second American Amateur championship. The USGA's reluctance to hold its premier event here was born principally of the fear that it was not close enough to a major city. The anxiety has happily been proved to be misplaced for there is no finer setting nor more demanding an examination of a golfer's skills.

Sprawling along the rocky shores and cliffs of Carmel Bay, only just round the headland from that other jewel, Cypress Point, it possesses some quite stupendous holes and particularly the sequence between the fourth and tenth.

Of these, the pick are the tiny seventh, a mere 110yd (100m) to a small green nestling amid the spray-soaked rocks of the Pacific; the eighth with its awesome second shot over a chasm in the cliffs; and the ninth and 10th, two classic, long pars fours hugging the sweep of the bay on fairways sloping teasingly towards the ocean.

Elsewhere, the course winds up to the fringes of the Del Monte Forest, where millionaires have their week-end retreats, before swooping down again to that marvellous finishing hole, 548yd (499m) of it bending gently left along the line of the shore with its rock-strewn beach beckoning disaster. A frequent cloak of fog, rolling in from the sea merely heightens the drama.

Overleaf: Pebble Beach's eighth green and, beyond, the majestic sweep of Carmel Bay.

THE CARD					
Hole	Yard	Par	Hole	Yards	Par
1	379	4	10	424	4
2	506	5	11	382	4
3	395	4	12	204	3
4	327	4	13	393	4
5	170	3	14	565	5
6	516	5	15	395	4
7	110	3	16	403	4
8	433	4	17	209	3
9	467	4	18	548	5
	3,302	36		3,523	36

Total: 6,825yd (6,211m) Par 72

Royal County Down. The 10th hole, clubhouse and, beyond, the Mountains of Mourne.

Royal County Down, Newcastle, Northern Ireland.

In times when it is nothing to spend £1 million on the construction of a new golf course in some parts of the world, it is hard to believe that when the County Down club was formed in 1889, Old Tom Morris was entrusted with its layout on a budget that was 'not to exceed £4'. One can only say now that it was a good investment!

It lies in one of the loveliest settings imaginable, the great Mountains of Mourne brooding to the south just beyond the little town of Newcastle and the broad, sandy beaches of Dundrum Bay stretching on its eastern flank.

Certainly there have been alterations to the course over the years, but such is its almost regal splendour amid the sandhills, broken here and there by vivid clumps of gorse, that the granting of the Royal charter in 1908 could hardly have been more worthy. At the best part of 7,000yd (6,370m) in length it is un-

doubtedly a 'big man's course' and deserving of the very best occasions.

Thirty miles (48km) south of Belfast, it is nevertheless a little 'tucked away' as well as being a victim of the festering Irish troubles. For that reason, plans to take the Walker Cup there in the 1970s had to be abandoned. Royal County Down did however stage the Curtis Cup in 1968 and with the gorse then a blaze of summer yellow, the Americans went home enchanted as well as victorious.

The women indeed have been particularly faithful patrons, the British championship first being played there in 1899 when May Hezlet, crowned Irish champion only the week before, won at the tender age of 17. 'Cecil' Leitch (1920), Thion de la Chaune (now Madame René Lacoste) in 1927, Wanda Morgan (1935), the Vicomtesse de Saint-Sauveur (1950) and Brigitte Varangot (1963) also all departed victorious. For the men, Michael Bonallack completed a hat-trick of Amateur championship triumphs there in 1970.

If the course has a weakness, it lies in the relatively high proportion of blind tee shots, perhaps the most fierce of which is that over a high ridge to the second fairway. There are also only two par fours of less than 400 yd (364m) one of which, the 16th, can just about be driven, while three of the four par threes measure 200yd (132km) and more.

Yet somehow Royal County Down seldom seems a 'slog' for the ground is invariably firm, the fairways twist and turn through the valleys between the sandhills and always there is the magnificence of the scenery.

THE CARD					
Hole	Yard	Par	Hole	Yards	Par
1	512	5	10	200	3
2	424	4	11	441	4
3	468	4	12	503	5
4	211	3	13	445	4
5	440	4	14	216	3
6	394	4	15	454	4
7	137	3	16	267	4
8	427	4	17	420	4
9	488	5	18	548	5
	3,501	36		3,494	36
		Total: 6,995yd (6,366m) par 72			

Royal Liverpool, Hoylake, England.

Like Carnoustie, Royal Liverpool no longer appears on the Open championship roster, a fault neither of the club nor the course. There is simply not the room to accommodate the attendant circus that has become so much a part of what now ranks as one of Britain's, indeed the world's, great sporting occasions.

This is a pity for Hoylake is often referred to as the 'St. Andrews of England'. It dates back to 1869, and of the seaside courses is second only to Westward Ho! in seniority. It staged the first Amateur championship in 1885 and, in 1902, the Open which Alex Herd won using the new rubber-cored ball, thereby changing the whole course of golf history.

Later, in 1921, Britain's amateurs met the United States at Hoylake in an international match from which stemmed the Walker Cup while it was also here in 1930 that Bobby Jones added the Open championship to the Amateur title he had collected earlier at St. Andrews on the way to completing his legendary Grand Slam.

Hoylake was, as well, the home of two famous golfing sons: John Ball, the first amateur and the first Englishman to win the Open in 1890, and Harold Hilton, another amateur who won the Open twice, the Amateur four times and in 1911 was the last Englishman to take the American Amateur.

Everything about Royal Liverpool is steeped in history, though to look out from the big, club-room window across the broad expanse of links, a row of

The 11th hole at Hoylake as spectators follow the 1983 Walker Cup match between Britain and the United States.

houses now on its far flank, one would never suspect the severity of the challenge. It looks too flat and featureless.

Only at the turn, where for six holes the course climbs among the dunes beside the Dee estuary, with the distant mountains of North Wales rising on its far side, does one find the severe undulations associated with links golf. Yet it does not mean weakness in the rest.

The most unusual feature here is the practice ground, which is out of bounds, guarded by a low bank and lying between the first and 16th holes. The second shots at both are therefore fraught with peril, though the fearlessness of Roberto de Vicenzo, who cut the corner at the 16th to secure a birdie four in the last round, was crucial in his popular Open victory of 1967. It was the last to be played at Hoylake, once part of a racecourse; hence the names of the first and 18th holes, respectively 'Course' and 'Stand'.

THE CARD

Hole		Yards	Par	Hole		Yards	Par
1	Course	428	4	10	Dee	409	4
2	Road	369	4	11	Alps	200	3
3	Long	505	5	12	Hilbre	454	4
4	Cop	195	3	13	Rushes	157	3
5	Telegraph	449	4	14	Field	512	5
6	Briars	423	4	15	Lake	460	4
7	Dowie	200	3	16	Dun	533	5
8	Far	519	5	17	Royal	418	4
9	Punchbowl	393	4	18	Stand	395	4
		3,481	36			3,538	36

Total: 7,019yd (6,387m) Par 72

Royal Melbourne, Victoria, Australia.

There are two courses at Royal Melbourne: the West, which was designed by Alister Mackenzie (of Augusta National and Cypress Point fame) and the East, which was the work of his pupil, Alex Russell, the Australian Open champion of 1924. While the West is considered the superior of the two, there is precious little in it and on the big occasion, like an Australian Open or, for instance, the 1959 Canada Cup (now World Cup) a composite of the two courses is used, drawing on the best of both.

The result is one of the outstanding

courses in the world, Peter Thomson maintaining that very possibly it is the best of all and Ben Crenshaw placing it in his top three. The sandy duneland was the perfect canvas for such an artist as Mackenzie and he made the most of it against a background of she-oaks, tea trees, heather and bracken.

Yet Royal Melbourne's reputation has been due as much as anything to its former head greenkeeper, Claude Crockford, who nurtured the course for some 40 years, beginning in 1934, not long after it had opened. It was the greens to which he devoted much love and care and nowadays there is probably nowhere else with such devilishly quick putting surfaces.

In 1974, Lee Trevino was scathingly critical of them, maintaining that they were so 'unputtable' that he vowed never to return, and never has. Yet four years later Hale Irwin completed the course in 64, though he subsequently tended to regard that as a fluke.

As with many of the great courses around the world, the bunkers are both magnificently big and deep – huge craters dug out by horse and scoop, which Crockford always maintained was the only lasting method of construction.

The 1959 Canada Cup was the first occasion on which big-time golf came to Australia and victory at the Royal Melbourne by the home pair of Peter Thomson and Kel Nagle lit the fuse for the years ahead. In 1968 Royal Melbourne was also host to the world amateur team championship for the Eisenhower Trophy and it has also been a regular venue for the Australian Open and Amateur championships.

Perhaps the hallmark of its greatness lies in the wide fluctuation of scoring – from that 64 by Irwin and a 65 once by Sam Snead, to 105 by a certain Indonesian.

Royal Melbourne's greens are among the fastest in the world.

THE CARD

Hole	Yard	Par	Hole	Yards	Par
1	424	4	10	460	4
2	480	5	11	455	4
3	333	4	12	433	4
4	440	4	13	354	4
5	176	3	14	470	4
6	428	4	15	383	4
7	148	3	16	210	3
8	305	4	17	575	5
9	440	4	18	432	4
	3,174	35		3,772	36

Total: 6,946yd (6,321m) Par 71.

St. Andrews, Fife, Scotland.

St. Andrews is the home of the Royal and Ancient, golf's governing authority, though in itself a private club. The R & A headquarters is its much-photographed greystone clubhouse immediately behind the first tee of the Old course, which, contrary to popular assumption, is not owned by the R & A at all but (like the other St. Andrews' courses, the New, Eden and Jubilee) belongs to the North-East Fife District Council. Each is open to the public on payment of a green fee.

The Old is nevertheless *the* course and it has now staged more Open championships (23) than any other in current use. Once it consisted of 22 holes – 11 out and then an exact retracing of the steps playing the holes in the opposite direc-

tion. But by the early 1830s it had been reduced to nine each way with different flag positions for the inward half.

Even now, only the first, ninth, 17th and 18th holes have their own greens. All the rest are doubles, the second sharing with the 16th, the third with the 15th and each combination, by a quirk of coincidence, adding up to 18. Quite the most intriguing aspect of St. Andrews is how little has changed. Apart from a new tee here and there over the years the test for Severiano Ballesteros in 1984 was much the same as it had been for Bob Martin and David Strath when they tied in 1876.

No course in the world has stood the test of time so unwaveringly. St. Andrews was not built by the hand of man but created by nature some 4–500 years ago. Even the bunkers were in many cases originally created by sheep bur-

One of the features of the Old course at St. Andrews is its double greens. Here players on the 14th wait for those on the fourth to putt out.

rowing into the dunes for protection from the winds.

Many of them have names, like Hell, which guards the route to the 14th; the Principal's Nose in the middle of the 16th fairway; Strath immediately in front of the 11th green and Cockle, fronting the seventh. Even those who play the course regularly can come upon a bunker they never knew existed.

The Old course is more frustrating than difficult. The double greens are enormous and with their great swirls and undulations the art lies in hitting the approach shots close enough to avoid three, four and even five-putting. Bobby Jones, on his first visit 1921, tore up his card in despair. By comparison, Tony Lema won the 1964 Open despite leaving himself only 36 hours in which to aquaint himself with the course.

Yet the 'old lady' as it is sometimes called, has never submitted to a score of lower than 65. Often there have been threats, notably when Tony Jacklin went out in 29 in the first round of the 1970 Open; then it was a storm which intervened . . . but always there is something.

THE CARD							
Hole		Yards	Par	Hole		Yards	Par
1	Burn	370	4	10	Bobby Jones	342	4
2	Dyke	411	4	11	High	172	3
3	Cartgate	398	4	12	Heathery	316	4
4	Ginger Beer	463	4	13	Hole O'Cross	425	4
5	Hole O'Cross	564	5	14	Long	567	5
6	Heathery	416	4	15	Cartgate	413	4
7	High	372	4	16	Corner of the Dyke	382	4
8	Short	178	3	17	Road Hole	461	4
9	End	356	4	18	Tom Morris	354	4
		3,528	36			3,432	36

Total: 6,960yd (6,334m) Par 72.

Below right: The approach to the seventh green on the Old course at Sunningdale.

Sunningdale, Surrey, England.

Some of the loveliest courses in England are those on the heath where the land is full of bracken and heather, gorse and broom, pine and silver birch. The soil is light, even sandy and it is ideal for golf all the year round, unlike some of the parkland courses which tend to get heavy in the winter rains.

High on the list is Sunningdale, on the Surrey–Berkshire border west of London. Among its neighbours are Wentworth and The Berkshire and while there are others of similar type, like Walton Heath in the same county, Woodhall Spa in Lincolnshire, Hollinwell in Nottinghamshire and Gleneagles in Scotland, Sunningdale marginally outranks them all.

There are two courses, the Old and the New, and if it is the former by which it is best known, there are not a few who maintain that the New is better, certainly tougher. New tees have now extended the Old beyond 6,500yd (5,915m) but it is control that is needed more than length.

All the fairways are tightly bordered by heather and trees, and other than the first and 18th, which run side by side in opposite directions, each hole is isolated from the rest giving the golfer the feeling that he is alone on the course. In the 80-odd years since Willie Park, son of the very first Open winner and a champion twice himself, made the original design the panorama has become wooded, giving protection from the wind.

There are nevertheless some exposed parts, notably from the high tees at the fifth and 10th; but both offer enchanting views along the fairways far below while there is the further incentive before driving off at the 11th of hot sausages sizzling in the frying pan at the Half Way House.

Something even stronger may not come amiss for the 11th is one of the great short par fours: a right-hand dog leg behind some trees leading to a green rather like an upturned saucer and the very devil on which to lay the ball close as the golfer struggles to choose between the little run-up or the short, lofted pitch.

It is one of several birdie opportunities, for both the third and ninth are driveable par fours and not one of the par fives is consistently out of range in two by the best player on his game. A 66 by Bobby Jones in a qualifying round for the 1926 Open, while no longer a course record, is still regarded as 'the perfect round of golf' – all fours and threes, 33 shots and 33 putts.

	THE CARD				
Hole	Yard	Par	Hole	Yards	Par
1	494	5	10	478	5
2	484	5	11	325	4
3	296	4	12	451	4
4	161	3	13	185	3
5	410	4	14	509	5
6	415	4	15	226	3
7	402	4	16	438	4
8	192	3	17	421	4
9	267	4	18	432	4
	3,121	36		3,465	36

Total: 6,586yd (5,993m) Par 72.

Tournament Players Club, Ponte Vedra Beach, Florida, USA.

When Jerry Pate won the American Tournament Players' championship here in 1982, his first action after holing the winning putt was to throw Deane Beman, the PGA Tour commissioner, and Pete Dye, the golf course architect, into the lake beside the 18th hole. It may have been a 'put up job' but it also reflected an opinion of one of the most contentiously designed golf courses in recent times.

Compared to the 100 and more acres of the average course, only 45 at the TPC, which is also the headquarters of the PGA Tour, need to be maintained. The rest, winding through an extensive area of oak, pine and palm, can be left to nature as the island fairways are bordered by long stretches of sandy waste, rather in the manner of Pine Valley.

However the TPC is much more than just a long and difficult golf course. It fulfills the vision of Beman, who wanted, and has now got, the first stadium-built course – one that enables vast numbers of spectators to see the golf from natural vantage points rather than specially erected stands. It is without question the world's best course for watching play and has set a fashion for the future.

Twenty miles (32km) from Jacksonville and just across the road from Sawgrass, which for many years was the home of the Tournament Players' cham-

Overleaf: One of the holes where the spectators gather eagerly at the Tournament Players' Club, Sawgrass: the short 17th. The tee shot is played from the bottom left-hand corner of the picture.

pionship, the course was opened within two years of construction work beginning in February, 1979, and the impact, or rather explosion, it caused was instant.

Immediately following Pate's victory, many leading players signed a petition to the effect that the course was 'too difficult', criticizing particularly some of the severely sloping greens. Some modification has been made to the putting surfaces while even the sandy wastes are in places now raked.

In 1984 Fred Couples promptly bettered Pate's winning total of 280 by three strokes, one of his rounds being a 64, and while this may have been exceptional, 13 players nevertheless beat par over the four rounds.

Most of the holes have water threatening them somewhere and none is more dramatic than the 133yd (121m) 17th where the sleepered green is set in a lake, entirely surrounded by water apart from a narrow causeway at its rear. It is an 'all or nothing' shot and repeatedly confounds even the best.

THE CARD					
Hole	Yard	Par	Hole	Yards	Par
1	388	4	10	395	4
2	511	5	11	529	5
3	162	3	12	336	4
4	360	4	13	172	3
5	454	4	14	438	4
6	381	4	15	426	4
7	439	4	16	497	5
8	215	3	17	132	3
9	582	5	18	440	4
	3,492	36		3,365	36
Total: 6,857yd (6,240m) Par 72					

Turnberry, Ayrshire, Scotland.

Turnberry is the most spectacular of all the courses on the Open championship roster, though its inclusion is only recent. Its debut in 1977 brought a classic confrontation between Tom Watson and Jack Nicklaus, Watson squeezing home with a final round of 65 to Nicklaus' 66 after they had each played the first three identically in 68, 70 and 65.

No stage could have been more fitting for such a fight to the death, for the backcloth is breathtaking: a rock-strewn and rugged coastline looking west across the mouth of the Firth of Clyde towards the tumbling mountains of the isle of Arran, the low outline of the Mull of Kintyre on the horizon and always, or nearly always, Ailsa Craig, a great bulging, dome-shaped rock climbing out of the depths of the sea.

It is an old saying in these parts that if one can see Ailsa Craig it is going to rain and, if you cannot, it is raining! Certainly at the time of the equinox, when the daylight hours equal those of the night, Turnberry can be the most wild and windy place. But at other times, as the sky glows like fire in an incomparable sunset, the scene is utterly tranquil.

There are two courses, the Ailsa and the Arran. The former is the championship test, almost 7,000yd (6,370m) in length and nearly half of it following the line of the shore towards the lighthouse which watches over the ninth hole with its spectacular drive from a tee perched on an outcrop of rock. With the sea surging at its foot and jagged cliffs to be carried, it is a moment every golfer relishes.

Yet Turnberry, with its famous hotel standing on high ground and commanding the most lovely views, was nearly lost. During the Second World War it was a landing strip for RAF Coastal Command and many of the fairways disappeared under tarmac, the remnants of which can still be found today.

Mackenzie Ross, the Scottish architect, was put in charge of its reconstruction and produced an even better course than previously. More adjustments were made before the 1977 Open and more again in readiness for the next in 1986. Only the keenest eye would nevertheless detect them, others perhaps in the reduction in length of the fifth hole, once a par five, now a four.

Turnberry has hosted many notable events, not least the 1963 Walker Cup match, when the USA came from behind to win, the 1961 Amateur championship, when Michael Bonallack began his long run of success and the 1983 Amateur when Philip Parkin became the first British player in 60 years to defeat a member of the American Walker Cup team in the final.

THE CARD							
Hole		Yards	Par	Hole		Yards	Par
1	Ailsa Craig	362	4	10	Dinna Fouter	452	4
2	Mak Siccar	428	4	11	Maidens	177	3
3	Blaw Wearie	462	4	12	Monument	447	4
4	Woe-be-Tide	167	3	13	Tickly Tap	411	4
5	Fin' me oot	450	4	14	Tisk-an-Hope	440	4
6	Tappie Toorie	222	3	15	Ca Canny	209	3
7	Roon the Ben	528	5	16	Wee Burn	409	4
8	Goat Fell	427	4	17	Lang Whang	500	5
9	Bruce's Castle	455	4	18	Ailsa Home	431	4
		3,501	35			3,476	35

Total: 6,977yd (6,349m) Par 70

Winged Foot, Mamaroneck, New York.

Unlike in Britain, where the Open is traditionally held on a links, the US Open seldom goes anywhere near the coast, the USGA preferring to keep it within easy range of the big cities. While a number of these inland courses tend to have a 'sameness' about them, Winged Foot stands apart.

It takes its name from the New York Athletic Club, some of whose members helped in its foundation. There are two courses, the West and the East, both designed by A. W. Tillinghast, and while there is often argument as to which is the better of the two, it is the West which has always been chosen for the big occasion.

'Big' is undoubtedly the word for it, for it was not until 1984, when Fuzzy Zoeller and the Australian, Greg Norman, tied on 276 before Zoeller won the play-off, that anybody had beaten the par of 280 for the four rounds of a US Open. In 1929 Bobby Jones and Al Espinosa also tied, on 294, before Jones won the play-off; in 1952 Billy Casper putted like a wizard for a score of 282; and in 1974 Hale Irwin returned 287, seven over par, and still won by two strokes.

It is the last five holes that best sum up Winged Foot. Each is a par four but the shortest is 417yd (380m). Together they stretch for almost 1¼ miles (2km) and have an average length of 435yd (396m), which is extremely taxing at any time and especially so at the height of a champion-

ship. Some would argue that it is too taxing and that the course therefore lacks variety, or certainly subtlety.

However the par threes are nicely balanced and the two par fives, the fifth and 12th, demand two supreme strokes if they are to be reached in two. It is hardly surprising therefore that Winged Foot has bred so many good players.

At one time it was able to boast both the US Open and Amateur champions, Craig Wood, the resident professional, winning the Open in 1941 following the victory the previous autumn of Dick Chapman in the Amateur. Later Claude Harmon, who succeeded Wood, went on to become Masters champion of 1948 while Dick Mayer, the Open champion of 1957, had been an amateur member.

Unusually for US courses, the bunkers are sometimes deeper than man himself, hemming in the greens and offering little respite before that murderous mile leading back to the sanctuary of the attractive, low-gabled clubhouse.

THE CARD					
Hole	Yard	Par	Hole	Yards	Par
1	446	4	10	180	3
2	411	4	11	433	4
3	216	3	12	535	5
4	460	4	13	212	3
5	515	5	14	418	4
6	324	4	15	417	4
7	161	3	16	452	4
8	442	4	17	444	4
9	456	4	18	448	4
	3,431	35		3,539	35
Total: 6,970yd (6,343m) Par 70.					

A bunker lurking in wait beside Winged Foot's ninth green with the clubhouse half hidden by the trees.

5 CHAMPIONSHIP RESULTS

THE OPEN CHAMPIONSHIP

(denotes an amateur)*

YEAR	VENUE	WINNER	SCORE
1860	Prestwick	Willie Park	174
1861	Prestwick	Tom Morris Snr	163
1862	Prestwick	Tom Morris Snr	163
1863	Prestwick	Willie Park	168
1864	Prestwick	Tom Morris Snr	167
1865	Prestwick	Andrew Strath	162
1866	Prestwick	Willie Park	169
1867	Prestwick	Tom Morris Snr	170
1868	Prestwick	Tom Morris Jnr	157
1869	Prestwick	Tom Morris Jnr	154
1870	Prestwick	Tom Morris Jnr	149
1871	No competition		
1872	Prestwick	Tom Morris Jnr	166
1873	St Andrews	Tom Kidd	179
1874	Musselburgh	Mungo Park	159
1875	Prestwick	Willie Park	166
1876	St Andrews	Bob Martin	176
1877	Musselburgh	Jamie Anderson	160
1878	Prestwick	Jamie Anderson	157
1879	St Andrews	Jamie Anderson	169
1880	Musselburgh	Bob Ferguson	162
1881	Prestwick	Bob Ferguson	170
1882	St Andrews	Bob Ferguson	171
1883	Musselburgh	Willie Fernie	159
1884	Prestwick	Jack Simpson	160
1885	St Andrews	Bob Martin	171
1886	Musselburgh	David Brown	157
1887	Prestwick	Willie Park Jnr	161
1888	St Andrews	Jack Burns	171
1889	Musselburgh	Willie Park Jnr (play-off with Andrew Kirkaldy)	155
1890	Prestwick	*John Ball	164
1891	St Andrews	Hugh Kirkaldy	166
1892	Muirfield	*Harold Hilton (championship extended to 72 holes)	305
1893	Prestwick	Willie Auchterlonie	322
1894	Sandwich	J.H. Taylor	326
1895	St Andrews	J.H. Taylor	322
1896	Muirfield	Harry Vardon (play-off with J.H. Taylor)	316
1897	Hoylake	*Harold Hilton	314
1898	Prestwick	Harry Vardon	307
1899	Sandwich	Harry Vardon	310
1900	St Andrews	J.H. Taylor	309
1901	Muirfield	James Braid	309
1902	Hoylake	Alex Herd	307
1903	Prestwick	Harry Vardon	300
1904	Sandwich	Jack White	296
1905	St Andrews	James Braid	318
1906	Muirfield	James Braid	300
1907	Hoylake	Arnaud Massy (France)	312
1908	Prestwick	James Braid	291
1909	Deal	J.H. Taylor	295
1910	St Andrews	James Braid	299
1911	Sandwich	Harry Vardon (play-off with Arnaud Massy)	303
1912	Muirfield	Ted Ray	295
1913	Hoylake	J.H. Taylor	304
1914	Prestwick	Harry Vardon	306
1915–1919	No competition		
1920	Deal	George Duncan	303
1921	St Andrews	Jock Hutchison (US) (play-off with Roger Wethered)	296
1922	Sandwich	Walter Hagen (US)	300
1923	Troon	Arthur Havers	295
1924	Hoylake	Walter Hagen (US)	301
1925	Prestwick	Jim Barnes (US)	300
1926	Royal Lytham	*Bobby Jones Jnr (US)	291
1927	St Andrews	*Bobby Jones Jnr (US)	285
1928	Sandwich	Walter Hagen (US)	292
1929	Muirfield	Walter Hagen (US)	292
1930	Hoylake	*Bobby Jones Jnr (US)	291
1931	Carnoustie	Tommy Armour (US)	296
1932	Prince's	Gene Sarazen (US)	283
1933	St Andrews	Densmore Shute (US) (play-off with Craig Wood)	292
1934	Sandwich	Henry Cotton	283
1935	Muirfield	Alf Perry	283
1936	Hoylake	Alf Padgham	287
1937	Carnoustie	Henry Cotton	290
1938	Sandwich	Reg Whitcombe	295
1939	St Andrews	Dick Burton	290
1940–1945	No competition		
1946	St Andrews	Sam Snead (US)	290
1947	Hoylake	Fred Daly	293
1948	Muirfield	Henry Cotton	284
1949	Sandwich	Bobby Locke (Sth Africa) (play-off with Harry Bradshaw)	283
1950	Troon	Bobby Locke (Sth Africa)	279
1951	Royal Portrush	Max Faulkner	285
1952	Royal Lytham	Bobby Locke (Sth Africa)	287
1953	Carnoustie	Ben Hogan (US)	282
1954	Royal Birkdale	Peter Thomson (Australia)	283
1955	St Andrews	Peter Thomson (Australia)	281
1956	Hoylake	Peter Thomson (Australia)	286
1957	St Andrews	Bobby Locke (Sth Africa)	279
1958	Royal Lytham	Peter Thomson (Australia) (play-off with David Thomas)	278
1959	Muirfield	Gary Player (Sth Africa)	284
1960	St Andrews	Kel Nagle (Australia)	278
1961	Royal Birkdale	Arnold Palmer (US)	284
1962	Troon	Arnold Palmer (US)	276
1963	Royal Lytham	Bob Charles (New Zealand) (play-off with Phil Rodgers)	277
1964	St Andrews	Tony Lema (US)	279
1965	Royal Birkdale	Peter Thomson (Australia)	285
1966	Muirfield	Jack Nicklaus (US)	282
1967	Hoylake	Roberto de Vicenzo (Argentina)	278

UNITED STATES OPEN

(Players from the US unless otherwise stated. *denotes an amateur)*

YEAR	VENUE	WINNER	SCORE
1954	Baltusrol, NJ	Ed Furgol	284
1955	Olympic, Cal	Jack Fleck (play-off with Ben Hogan)	287
1956	Oak Hill, NY	Cary Middlecoff	281
1957	Inverness, Ohio	Dick Mayer (play-off with Cary Middlecoff)	282
1958	Southern Hills, Okla	Tommy Bolt	283
1959	Winged Foot, NY	Billy Casper	282
1960	Cherry Hills, Colo	Arnold Palmer	280
1961	Oakland Hills, Mich	Gene Littler	281
1962	Oakmont, Pa	Jack Nicklaus (play-off with Arnold Palmer)	283
1963	Brookline, Mass	Julius Boros (play-off with Jacky Cupit and Arnold Palmer)	293
1964	Congressional, Wash, DC.	Ken Venturi	278
1965	Bellerive, Miss	Gary Player (Sth Africa) (play-off with Kel Nagle)	282
1966	Olympic, Cal	Billy Casper (play-off with Arnold Palmer)	278
1967	Baltusrol, NJ	Jack Nicklaus	275
1968	Oak Hill NY	Lee Trevino	275
1969	Champions, Tex	Orville Moody	281
1970	Hazeltine, Minn	Tony Jacklin (GB)	281
1971	Merion, Pa	Lee Trevino (play-off with Jack Nicklaus)	280
1972	Pebble Beach, Cal	Jack Nicklaus	290
1973	Oakmont, Pa	Johnny Miller	279
1974	Winged Foot NY	Hale Irwin	287
1975	Medinah, Ill	Lou Graham (play-off with John Mahaffey)	287
1976	Atlanta, Ga	Jerry Pate	277
1977	Southern Hills, Okla	Hubert Green	278
1978	Cherry Hills, Colo	Andy North	285
1979	Inverness, Ohio	Hale Irwin	284
1980	Baltusrol, NJ	Jack Nicklaus	272
1981	Merion, Pa	David Graham (Australia)	273
1982	Pebble Beach, Cal	Tom Watson	282
1983	Oakmont, Pa	Larry Nelson	280
1984	Winged Foot, NY	Fuzzy Zoeller (play-off with Greg Norman)	276
1985	Oakland Hills, Mich	Andy North	279

UNITED STATES PGA CHAMPIONSHIP

(Players from US unless otherwise stated.)

YEAR	VENUE	WINNER	SCORE
1916	Siwanoy, NY	Jim Barnes	
1919	Engineers, NY	Jim Barnes	
1920	Flossmoor, Ill	Jock Hutchison	
1921	Inwood, NY	Walter Hagen	
1922	Oakmont, Pa	Gene Sarazen	
1923	Pelham, NY	Gene Sarazen	
1924	French Lick, Ind	Walter Hagen	
1925	Olympia Fields, Ill	Walter Hagen	
1926	Salisbury, NY	Walter Hagen	
1927	Cedar Crest, Tex	Walter Hagen	
1928	Baltimore, Md	Leo Diegel	
1929	Hillcrest, Cal	Leo Diegel	
1930	Fresh Meadow, NY	Tommy Armour	
1931	Wannamoisett, RI	Tom Creavy	
1932	Keller, Minn	Olin Dutra	
1933	Blue Mound, Wis	Gene Sarazen	
1934	Park, NY	Paul Runyan	
1935	Twin Hills, Okla	Johnny Revolta	
1936	Pinehurst, NC	Densmore Shute	
1937	Pittsburgh, Pa	Densmore Shute	
1938	Shawnee, Pa	Paul Runyan	
1939	Pomonok, NY	Henry Picard	
1940	Hershey, Pa	Byron Nelson	
1941	Cherry Hills, Colo	Vic Ghezzi	
1942	Seaview, NJ	Sam Snead	
1944	Manito, Wash	Bob Hamilton	
1945	Morraine, Ohio	Byron Nelson	
1946	Portland, Ore	Ben Hogan	
1947	Plum Hollow, Mich	Jim Ferrier	
1948	Norwood Hills, Miss	Ben Hogan	
1949	Hermitage, Va	Sam Snead	
1950	Scioto, Ohio	Chandler Harper	
1951	Oakmont, Pa	Sam Snead	
1952	Big Spring, Ky	Jim Turnesa	
1953	Birmingham, Mich	Walter Burkemo	
1954	Keller, Minn	Chick Harbert	
1955	Meadowbrook, Mich	Doug Ford	
1956	Blue Hill, Mass	Jack Burke	
1957	Miami Valley, Ohio	Lionel Hebert	
1958	Llanerch, Pa	Dow Finsterwald (championship changed to stroke play)	276
1959	Minneapolis, Minn	Bob Rosburg	277
1960	Firestone, Ohio	Jay Hebert	281
1961	Olympia Fields, Ill	Jerry Barber (play-off with Don January)	277
1962	Aronimink, Pa	Gary Player (Sth Africa)	278
1963	Dallas, Tex	Jack Nicklaus	279
1964	Columbus, Ohio	Bobby Nichols	271
1965	Laurel Valley, Pa	Dave Marr	280
1966	Firestone, Ohio	Al Geiberger	280
1967	Columbine, Colo	Don January (play-off with Don Massengale)	281
1968	Pecan Valley, Tex	Julius Boros	281
1969	Dayton, Ohio	Ray Floyd	276
1970	Southern Hills Okla	Dave Stockton	279
1971	PGA National, Fla	Jack Nicklaus	281
1972	Oakland Hills, Mich	Gary Player (Sth Africa)	281
1973	Canterbury, Ohio	Jack Nicklaus	277
1974	Tanglewood, NC	Lee Trevino	276
1975	Firestone, Ohio	Jack Nicklaus	276
1976	Congressional, Md	Dave Stockton	281
1977	Pebble Beach, Cal	Lanny Wadkins (play-off with Gene Littler)	282
1978	Oakmont, Pa	John Mahaffey (play-off with Jerry Pate and Tom Watson)	276

YEAR	VENUE	WINNER	SCORE
1979	Oakland Hills, Mich	David Graham (Australia) (play-off with Ben Crenshaw)	272
1980	Oak Hill, NY	Jack Nicklaus	274
1981	Atlanta, Ga	Larry Nelson	273

YEAR	VENUE	WINNER	SCORE
1982	Southern Hills, Okla	Raymond Floyd	272
1983	Riviera, Cal	Hal Sutton	274
1984	Shoal Creek, Ala	Lee Trevino	273
1985	Cherry Hills, Colo	Hubert Green	278

US MASTERS

(All played at Augusta National, Georgia.)

YEAR	WINNER	SCORE
1934	Horton Smith	284
1935	Gene Sarazen (play-off with Craig Wood)	282
1936	Horton Smith	285
1937	Byron Nelson	283
1938	Henry Picard	285
1939	Ralph Guldahl	279
1940	Jimmy Demaret	280
1941	Craig Wood	280
1942	Byron Nelson (play-off with Ben Hogan)	280
1943–1945	No competition	
1946	Herman Keiser	282
1947	Jimmy Demaret	281
1948	Claude Harman	279
1949	Sam Snead	282
1950	Jimmy Demaret	283
1951	Ben Hogan	280
1952	Sam Snead	286
1953	Ben Hogan	274
1954	Sam Snead (play-off with Ben Hogan)	289
1955	Cary Middlecoff	279
1956	Jack Burke Jnr	289
1957	Doug Ford	283
1958	Arnold Palmer	284
1959	Art Wall Jnr	284
1960	Arnold Palmer	282

YEAR	VENUE	WINNER	SCORE
1961		Gary Player (Sth Africa)	280
1962		Arnold Palmer (play-off with Gary Player and Dow Finsterwald)	280
1963		Jack Nicklaus	286
1964		Arnold Palmer	276
1965		Jack Nicklaus	271
1966		Jack Nicklaus (play-off with Tommy Jacobs and Gay Brewer)	288
1967		Gay Brewer	280
1968		Bob Goalby	277
1969		George Archer	281
1970		Billy Casper (play-off with Gene Littler)	279
1971		Charles Coody	279
1972		Jack Nicklaus	286
1973		Tommy Aaron	283
1974		Gary Player (Sth Africa)	278
1975		Jack Nicklaus	276
1976		Ray Floyd	271
1977		Tom Watson	276
1978		Gary Player (Sth Africa)	277
1979		Fuzzy Zoeller (play-off with Tom Watson and Ed Sneed)	280
1980		Severiano Ballesteros (Spain)	275
1981		Tom Watson	280
1982		Craig Stadler (play-off with Dan Pohl)	284
1983		Severiano Ballesteros (Spain)	280
1984		Ben Crenshaw	277
1985		Bernhard Langer (W. Germ)	282

AUSTRALIAN OPEN

(Players Australian unless otherwise stated.
* denotes an amateur)

YEAR	VENUE	WINNER	SCORE
1904	The Australian	*Hon Michael Scott (GB)	324
1905	Royal Melbourne	D. Soutar	330
1906	Royal Sydney	Carnegie Clark	322
1907	Royal Melbourne	*Hon Michael Scott (GB)	318
1908	The Australian	*Clyde Pearce	311
1909	Royal Melbourne	*Claude Felstead	316
1910	Royal Adelaide	Carnegie Clark	306
1911	Royal Sydney	Carnegie Clark	321
1912	Royal Melbourne	*Ivo Whitton	321
1913	Royal Melbourne	*Ivo Whitton	302
1914–1919	No competition		
1920	The Australian	Joe Kirkwood	290
1921	Royal Melbourne	A. le Fevre	295
1922	Royal Sydney	C. Campbell	307
1923	Royal Adelaide	T. Howard	301
1924	Royal Melbourne	*A. Russell	303
1925	The Australian	F. Popplewell	299
1926	Royal Adelaide	*Ivo Whitton	297
1927	Royal Melbourne	R. Stewart	297
1928	Royal Sydney	F. Popplewell	295
1929	Royal Adelaide	*Ivo Whitton	309
1930	Metropolitan	F. Eyre	306
1931	The Australian	*Ivo Whitton	301
1932	Royal Adelaide	* M.J. Ryan	296
1933	Royal Melbourne	M.L. Kelly	302
1934	Royal Sydney	W.J. Bolger	283
1935	Royal Adelaide	F. McMahon	293
1936	Metropolitan	Gene Sarazen (US)	282

YEAR	VENUE	WINNER	SCORE
1937	The Australian	G. Naismith	299
1938	Royal Adelaide	*Jim Ferrier	283
1939	Royal Melbourne	*Jim Ferrier	285
1940–1945	No competition		
1946	Royal Sydney	Ossie Pickworth	289
1947	Royal Queensland	Ossie Pickworth	285
1948	Kingston Heath	Ossie Pickworth	289
1949	The Australian	Eric Cremin	287
1950	Kooyonga	Norman von Nida	286
1951	Metropolitan	Peter Thomson	283
1952	Lake Karrinyup	Norman von Nida	278
1953	Royal Melbourne	Norman von Nida	278
1954	Kooyonga	Ossie Pickworth	280
1955	Gailes	Bobby Locke (Sth Africa)	290
1956	Royal Sydney	Bruce Crampton	289
1957	Kingston Heath	Frank Phillips	287
1958	Kooyonga	Gary Player (Sth Africa)	271
1959	The Australian	Kel Nagle	284
1960	Lake Karrinyup	*Bruce Devlin	282
1961	Victoria	Frank Phillips	275
1962	Royal Adelaide	Gary Player (Sth Africa)	281
1963	Royal Melbourne	Gary Player (Sth Africa)	278
1964	The Lakes	Jack Nicklaus (US)	287
1965	Kooyonga	Gary Player (Sth Africa)	264
1966	Royal Queensland	Arnold Palmer (US)	276
1967	Commonwealth	Peter Thomson	281
1968	Lake Karrinyup	Jack Nicklaus (US)	270

YEAR	VENUE	WINNER	SCORE
1969	Royal Sydney	Gary Player (Sth Africa)	288
1970	Kingston Heath	Gary Player (Sth Africa)	280
1971	Royal Hobart	Jack Nicklaus (US)	269
1972	Kooyonga	Peter Thomson	281
1973	Royal Queensland	J.C. Snead (US)	280
1974	Lake Karrinyup	Gary Player (Sth Africa)	279
1975	The Australian	Jack Nicklaus (US)	279

YEAR	VENUE	WINNER	SCORE
1976	The Australian	Jack Nicklaus (US)	286
1977	The Australian	David Graham	284
1978	The Australian	Jack Nicklaus (US)	284
1979	Metropolitan	Jack Newton	288
1980	The Lakes	Greg Norman	284
1981	Victoria	Bill Rogers (US)	282
1982	The Australian	Bob Shearer	287
1983	Kingston Heath	Peter Fowler	285
1984	Royal Melbourne	Tom Watson (US)	281
1985	Royal Melbourne	Greg Norman (54 holes)	212

SOUTH AFRICAN OPEN

(Players South African unless otherwise stated. * *denotes an amateur)*

YEAR	VENUE	WINNER	SCORE
1907	Kimberley	Lawrence Waters	147
1908	Johannesburg	George Fotheringham	163
1909	Potchefstroom	John Fotheringham	306
1910	Wynberg	George Fotheringham	315
1911	Durban	George Fotheringham	301
1912	Potchefstroom	George Fotheringham	305
1913	Kimberley	*J.A.W. Prentice	304
1914	Wynberg	George Fotheringham	299
1915–1918	No competition		
1919	Durban	W.H. Horne	320
1920	Johannesburg	L.B. Waters	302
1921	Port Elizabeth	Jack Brews (GB)	316
1922	Port Alfred	F. Jangle	310
1923	Royal Cape	Jack Brews (GB)	305
1924	Durban	B.H. Elkin	316
1925	Johannesburg	Sid Brews (GB)	295
1926	Port Elizabeth	Jack Brews (GB)	301
1927	Maccauvlei	Sid Brews (GB)	301
1928	Durban	Jack Brews (GB)	297
1929	Royal Cape	A. Tosh	315
1930	East London	Sid Brews (GB)	297
1931	Port Elizabeth	Sid Brews (GB)	302
1932	Mowbray	C. McIlvenny	304
1933	Maccauvlei	Sid Brews (GB)	297
1934	Port Elizabeth	Sid Brews (GB)	319
1935	Johannesburg	*Bobby Locke	296
1936	Royal Cape	*C.E. Olander	297
1937	East London	*Bobby Locke	288
1938	Maccauvlei	Bobby Locke	279
1939	Royal Durban	Bobby Locke	279
1940	Port Elizabeth	Bobby Locke	293
1941–1945	No competition		
1946	Royal Johannesburg	Bobby Locke	285
1947	Mowbray, Cape Town	*R.W. Glennie	293
1948	East London	*M. Janks	298

YEAR	VENUE	WINNER	SCORE
1949	Maccauvlei	Sid Brews (GB)	291
1950	Royal Durban	Bobby Locke	287
1951	Houghton	Bobby Locke	275
1952	Humewood	Sid Brews (GB)	300
1953	Royal Cape	*J.R. Boyd	302
1954	East London	*Reg Taylor	289
1955	Zwartkop	Bobby Locke	283
1956	Royal Durban	Gary Player	286
1957	Humewood	Harold Henning	289
1958	Bloemfontein	*A.A. Stewart	281
1959	Johannesburg	*Denis Hutchinson	282
1960	Mowbray	Gary Player	288
1961	East London	Retief Waltman	289
1962	Johannesburg	Harold Henning	285
1963	Royal Durban	Retief Waltman	281
1964	Bloemfontein	Alan Henning	278
1965	Cape Town	Gary Player	273
1966	Johannesburg	Gary Player	274
1967	East London	Gary Player	279
1968	Houghton	Gary Player	278
1969	Royal Durban	Gary Player	273
1970	Royal Durban	Tommy Horton (GB)	285
1971	Mowbray	Simon Hobday (Rhodesia)	276
1972	Royal Johannesburg	Gary Player	274
1973	Royal Durban	Bob Charles (NZ)	282
1974	Royal Johannesburg	Bobby Cole	272
1975	Mowbray	Gary Player	278
1976	Houghton and	Dale Hayes	287
	Royal Durban	Gary Player	280
	(Played twice due to date alteration)		
1977	Royal Johannesburg	Gary Player	273
1978	Mowbray	Hugh Baiocchi	285
1979	Houghton	Gary Player	279
1980	Durban CC	Bobby Cole	279
1981	Royal Johannesburg	Gary Player	272
1982	No competition		
1983	Royal Cape	Charles Bolling (US)	278
1984	Houghton	T. Johnstone (ZMB)	274
1985	Royal Durban	Gary Levenson	280

RYDER CUP

YEAR	VENUE	RESULT
1927	Worcester, Mass	US 9½, GB 2½
1929	Moortown, Leeds	GB 7, US 5
1931	Scioto, Ohio	US 9, GB 3
1933	Southport & Ainsdale, Lancs	GB 6½, US 5½
1935	Ridgewood, NJ	US 9, GB 3
1937	Southport & Ainsdale, Lancs	US 8, GB 4
1939–1945	Not played	
1947	Portland, Ore	US 11, GB 1
1949	Ganton, Yorks	US 7, GB 5
1951	Pinehurst, NC	US 9½, GB 2½
1953	Wentworth, Surrey	US 6½, GB 5½
1955	Palm Springs, Cal	US 8, GB 4
1957	Lindrick, Sheffield	GB 7½, US 4½

YEAR	VENUE	RESULT
1959	Palm Desert, Cal	US 8½, GB 3½
1961	Royal Lytham, Lancs	US 14½, GB 9½
1963	Atlanta, Ga	US 23, GB 9
1965	Royal Birkdale, Lancs	US 19½, GB 12½
1967	Houston, Tex	US 23½, GB 8½
1969	Royal Birkdale, Lancs	US 16, GB 16
1971	St Louis, Mo	US 18½, GB 13½
1973	Muirfield, Scotland	US 19, GB 13
1975	Laurel Valley, Pa	US 21, GB 11
1977	Royal Lytham, Lancs	US 12½, GB 7½
1979	Greenbrier, W Va	US 17, Europe 11
1981	Walton Heath, Surrey	US 18½, Europe 9½
1983	PGA National, Fla	US 14½, Europe 13½
1985	The Belfry, W. Midlands	US 11½, Europe 16½

WORLD CUP

YEAR	VENUE	WINNER
1953	Beaconsfield, Montreal	Argentina 287
1954	Laval sur le Lac, Montreal	Australia 556
1955	Columbia, Washington, USA	United States 560
1956	Wentworth, England	United States 567
1957	Kasumigaseki, Tokyo	Japan 557
1958	Club de Golf, Mexico City	Ireland 579
1959	Royal Melbourne, Australia	Australia 563
1960	Portmarnock, Dublin	United States 565
1961	Dorado Beach, Puerto Rico	United States 560
1962	Jockey Club, Buenos Aires	United States 557
1963	St Nom la Breteche, Paris	United States 482
1964	Royal Kaanapali, Hawaii	United States 554
1965	Club de Campo, Madrid	South Africa 571
1966	Yomiuri, Tokyo	United States 548

YEAR	VENUE	WINNER
1967	Club de Golf, Mexico City	United States 557
1968	Olgiata, Rome	Canada, 569
1969	Singapore Island	United States 552
1970	Jockey Club, Buenos Aires	Australia 544
1971	PGA National, Palm Beach, USA	United States 555
1972	Royal Melbourne, Australia	Taiwan 438
1973	Golf Nueva Andalucia, Spain	United States 558
1974	Lagunita, Venezuela	South Africa 554
1975	Navatanee, Bangkok	United States 554
1976	Mission Hills, Palm Springs USA	Spain 574
1977	Wack Wack, Manila	Spain 591
1978	Princeville Maka, Hawaii	United States 564
1979	Glyfada, Athens	United States 575
1980	El Rignon, Bogota	Canada 572
1981	No competition	
1982	Acapulco, Mexico	Spain 563
1983	Pondok Indah, Indonesia	United States 565
1984	Olgiata, Rome	Spain 414
1985	La Quinta, Cal	Canada 559

WALKER CUP

YEAR	VENUE	SCORE
1922	National Links, Long Island	US 8, GB & Ireland 4
1923	St Andrews, Scotland	US 6½, GB & Ireland 5½
1924	Garden City, NY	US 9, GB & Ireland 3
1926	St Andrews, Scotland	US 6½, GB & Ireland 5½
1928	Chicago GC, Ill	US 11, GB & Ireland 1
1930	Royal St Georges, Sandwich	US 10, GB & Ireland 2
1932	Country Club, Brooklyn, Mass.	US 9½, GB & Ireland 2½
1934	St Andrews, Scotland	US 9½, GB & Ireland 2½
1936	Pine Valley, NJ	US 10½, GB & Ireland 1½
1938	St Andrews, Scotland	GB & Ireland 7½, US 4½
1940–1946	No competition	
1947	St Andrews, Scotland	US 8, GB & Ireland 4
1949	Winged Foot NY	US 10, GB & Ireland 2
1951	Royal Birkdale, Lancs	US 7½, GB & Ireland 4½
1953	Kittansett, Mass	US 9, GB & Ireland 3

YEAR	VENUE	SCORE
1955	St Andrews, Scotland	US 10, GB & Ireland 2
1957	Minikahda, Minn	US 8½, GB & Ireland 3½
1959	Muirfield, Scotland	US 9, GB & Ireland 3
1961	Seattle, Washington	US 11, GB & Ireland 1
1963	Turnberry, Scotland	US 14, GB & Ireland 10
1965	Baltimore, Md	US 12, GB & Ireland 12
1967	Royal St Georges, Sandwich	US 15, GB & Ireland 9
1969	Milwaukee, Wis	US 13, GB & Ireland 11
1971	St Andrews, Scotland	GB & Ireland 13, US 11
1973	Brooklyn, Mass	US 14, GB & Ireland 10
1975	St Andrews, Scotland	US 15½, GB & Ireland 8½
1977	Shinnecock Hills, NY	US 16, GB & Ireland 8
1979	Muirfield, Scotland	US 15½, GB & Ireland 8½
1981	Cypress Point, Cal	US 15, GB & Ireland 9
1983	Royal Liverpool, England	US 13½, GB & Ireland 10½
1985	Pine Valley, NJ	US 13, GB 11

EISENHOWER TROPHY

(Men's world amateur team championship.)

YEAR	VENUE	WINNER
1958	St Andrews, Scotland	Australia 918
1960	Merion, US	United States 834
1962	Fuji, Japan	United States 854
1964	Olgiata, Italy	Gt Britain 895
1966	Mexico City	Australia 877
1968	Royal Melbourne, Australia	United States 868

YEAR	VENUE	WINNER
1970	Puerto de Hierro, Spain	United States 857
1972	Olivos, Argentina	United States 865
1974	Campo de Golf, Dominica	United States 888
1976	Penina, Portugal	Gt Britain 892
1978	Pacific Harbour, Fiji	United States 873
1980	Pinehurst No 2, United States	United States 848
1982	Lausanne, Switzerland	United States 859
1984	Royal Hong Kong	Japan 870

US WOMEN'S OPEN

(denotes an amateur)*

YEAR	VENUE	WINNER	SCORE
1946	Spokane, Washington	Patty Berg, (match-play)	5&4
1947	Starmount Forest CC	Betty Jameson	300
1948	Atlantic City CC	Mildred Zaharias	300
1949	Prince Georges G&CC	Louise Suggs	291
1950	Rolling Hills CC	Mildred Zaharias	291
1951	Druid Hills GC	Betsy Rawls	293
1952	Bala GC	Louise Suggs	284
1953	CC of Rochester	Betsy Rawls	302
1954	Salem CC	Mildred Zaharias	291
1955	Wichita CC	Fay Crocker	299
1956	Northland CC	Kathy Cornelius	302
1957	Winged Foot	Betsy Rawls	299
1958	Forest Lake CC	Mickey Wright	290
1959	Churchill Valley CC	Mickey Wright	287
1960	Worcester CC	Betsy Rawls	292
1961	Baltusrol GC	Mickey Wright	293
1962	Dunes Golf & Beach Club	Murle Lindstrom	301
1963	Kenwood CC	Mary Mills	289
1964	San Diego CC	Mickey Wright	290
1965	Alantic City CC	Carol Mann	290
1966	Hazeltine National GC	Sandra Spuzich	297
1967	Hot Springs, Virginia	*Catherine Lacoste (France)	294
1968	Moselem Springs GC	Susie Berning	289
1969	Scenic Hills CC	Donna Caponi	294
1970	Muskogee CC	Donna Caponi	287
1971	Kahkwa Club	JoAnne Carner	288
1972	Winged Foot	Susie Berning	299
1973	CC of Rochester	Susie Berning	290
1974	Le Grange CC	Sandra Haynie	295
1975	Atlantic City CC	Sandra Palmer	295
1976	Rolling Green GC	JoAnne Carner	292
1977	Hazeltine National	Hollis Stacy	292
1978	Indianapolis CC	Hollis Stacy	289
1979	Brooklawn CC	Jerilyn Britz	284
1980	Richland CC	Amy Alcott	280
1981	La Grange CC	Pat Bradley	279
1982	Del Paso, Sacramento	Janet Anderson	283
1983	Cedar Ridge, Tulsa	Jan Stephenson	290
1984	Salem, Mass	Hollis Stacy	290
1985	Baltusrol, NJ	Kathy Baker	280

BRITISH WOMEN'S OPEN

YEAR	VENUE	WINNER	SCORE
1976	Gosforth Park	Jenny Lee-Smith (GB)	299
1977	Lindrick	Vivien Saunders (GB)	306
1978	Foxhills	Janet Melville (GB)	310
1979	Southport & Ainsdale	Alison Sheard (Sth Africa)	301
1980	Wentworth East	Debbie Massey (US)	294
1981	Northumberland	Debbie Massey (US)	295
1982	Royal Birkdale	Marta Figuearas-Dotti (Spain)	296
1983	No competition		
1984	Woburn	Ayako Okamoto (Japan)	289
1985	Moor Park	Betsey King (US)	300

BRITISH WOMEN'S AMATEUR

(Players British unless otherwise stated.)

YEAR	VENUE	WINNER
1893	St Annes	Lady Margaret Scott
1894	Littlestone	Lady Margaret Scott
1895	Portrush	Lady Margaret Scott
1896	Hoylake	Amy Pascoe
1897	Gullane	Edith Orr
1898	Yarmouth	L. Thomson
1899	Newcastle, Co Down	May Hezlet
1900	Westward Ho!	Rhona Adair
1901	Aberdovey	Molly Graham
1902	Deal	May Hezlet
1903	Portrush	Rhona Adair
1904	Troon	Lottie Dod
1905	Cromer	B. Thompson
1906	Burnham	Mrs Kennion
1907	Newcastle, Co Down	May Hezlet
1908	St Andrews	M. Titterton
1909	Birkdale	Dorothy Campbell
1910	Westward Ho!	Mrs Grant Suttie
1911	Portrush	Dorothy Campbell
1912	Turnberry	Gladys Ravenscroft
1913	St Annes	Muriel Dodd
1914	Hunstanton	Cecil Leitch
1915–1918	No competition	
1919	Cancelled	
1920	Newcastle, Co Down	Cecil Leitch
1921	Turnberry	Cecil Leitch
1922	Prince's, Sandwich	Joyce Wethered
1923	Burnham	Doris Chambers
1924	Portrush	Joyce Wethered
1925	Troon	Joyce Wethered
1926	Harlech	Cecil Leitch
1927	Newcastle, Co Down	T. de la Chaume (France)
1928	Hunstanton	Nanette Le Blan (France)
1929	St Andrews	Joyce Wethered
1930	Formby	Diana Fishwick
1931	Portmarnock	Enid Wilson
1932	Saunton	Enid Wilson
1933	Gleneagles	Enid Wilson
1934	Royal Porthcawl	Helen Holm
1935	Newcastle, Co Down	Wanda Morgan
1936	Southport & Ainsdale	Pam Barton
1937	Turnberry	Jessie Anderson
1938	Burnham	Helen Holm
1939	Portrush	Pam Barton
1940–1945	No competition	
1946	Hunstanton	Jean Hetherington
1947	Gullane	Babe Zaharias (US)
1948	Royal Lytham	Louise Suggs (US)
1949	Harlech	Frances Stephens
1950	Newcastle, Co Down	Vicomtesse de St Sauveur (France)
1951	Broadstone	P.G. MacCann
1952	Troon	Moira Paterson
1953	Porthcawl	Marlene Stewart
1954	Ganton	Frances Stephens
1955	Portrush	Jessie Valentine
1956	Sunningdale	Margaret Smith
1957	Gleneagles	Philomena Garvey

YEAR	VENUE	WINNER
1958	Hunstanton	Jessie Valentine
1959	Ascot	Elizabeth Price
1960	Harlech	Barbara McIntire (US)
1961	Carnoustie	Marley Spearman
1962	Royal Birkdale	Marley Spearman
1963	Newcastle, Co Down	Brigitte Varangot (France)
1964	Prince's, Sandwich	Carol Sorenson (US)
1965	St Andrews	Brigitte Varangot (France)
1966	Ganton	Elizabeth Chadwick
1967	Harlech	Elizabeth Chadwick
1968	Walton Heath	Brigitte Varangot (France)
1969	Portrush	Catherine Lacoste (France)

YEAR	VENUE	WINNER
1970	Gullane	Dinah Oxley
1971	Alwoodley	Michelle Walker
1972	Hunstanton	Michelle Walker
1973	Carnoustie	Ann Irvin
1974	Royal Porthcawl	Carol Semple (US)
1975	St Andrews	Nancy Syms (US)
1976	Silloth	Cathy Panton
1977	Hillside	Angela Uzielli
1978	Notts	Edwina Kennedy (Australia)
1979	Nairn	Maureen Madill
1980	Woodhall Spa	Anne Sander (US)
1981	Caernarvonshire	Belle Robertson
1982	Walton Heath	Kitrina Douglas
1983	Silloth	Jill Thornhill
1984	Royal Troon	Jody Rosenthal (US)
1985	Ganton	Lilian Behan

ESPIRITO SANTO TROPHY

(Women's world amateur team championship.)

YEAR	VENUE	WINNER
1964	St Germain, France	France 588
1966	Mexico City CC	United States 580
1968	Victoria GC, Australia	United States 616

YEAR	VENUE	WINNER
1970	Club de Campo, Spain	United States 598
1972	Hindu CC, Argentina	United States 583
1974	Campo de Golf, Dominica	United States 620
1976	Vilamoura, Portugal	United States 605
1978	Pacific Harbour, Fiji	Australia 596
1980	Pinehurst No 2, USA	United States 588
1982	Geneva, Switzerland	United States 579
1984	Royal Hong Kong	United States 585

CURTIS CUP

YEAR	VENUE	RESULT
1932	Wentworth, Surrey	US 5½, GB & Ireland 3½
1934	Chevy Chase, Md	US 6½, GB & Ireland 2½
1936	Gleneagles, Scotland	US 4½, GB & Ireland 4½
1938	Essex CC, Mass.	US 5½, GB & Ireland 3½
1948	Royal Birkdale, Lancs	US 6½, GB & Ireland 2½
1950	Buffalo, NY	US 7½, GB & Ireland 1½
1952	Muirfield, Scotland	GB & Ireland 5, US 4
1954	Merion, Pa	US 6, GB & Ireland 3
1956	Prince's, England	GB & Ireland 5, US 4
1958	Brae Burn, Mass	GB & Ireland 4½, US 4½
1960	Lindrick, Yorks	US 6½, GB & Ireland 2½
1962	Broadmoor, Colorado Springs	US 8. GB & Ireland 1

YEAR	VENUE	WINNER	SCORE
1964	Royal Porthcawl, Wales		US 10½, GB & Ireland 7½
1966	Cascades, Hot Springs, VA		US 13, GB & Ireland 5
1968	Royal County Down, Ireland		US 10½, GB & Ireland 7½
1970	Brae Burn, Mass		US 11½, GB & Ireland 6½
1972	Western Gailes, Scotland		US 10, GB & Ireland 8
1974	San Francisco, Cal		US 13, GB & Ireland 5
1976	Royal Lytham, Lancs		US 11½, GB & Ireland 6½
1978	Apawamis, NY		US 12, GB & Ireland 6
1980	St Pierre, Chepstow, Wales		US 13, GB & Ireland 5
1982	Denver, Colo		US 14½, GB & Ireland 3½
1984	Muirfield, Scotland		US 9½, GB & Ireland 8½

GLOSSARY

Ace: A hole in one; most commonly achieved at a par three hole.

Address: Position a golfer adopts before commencing his swing.

Air Shot: Known by Americans as a 'whiff', it is an unsuccessful attempt to hit the ball with the clubhead.

Albatross: Three under par at one particular hole (i.e. holing out in two at a par five); also known as a double-eagle.

Approach: The shot to a green.

Apron: Area of short-cut grass just in front of the green.

Arc: The path of the hands, arms and club from the commencement to the completion of the swing.

As it lies: Position at which a ball comes to rest.

Away: A golfer is 'away' when it is his turn to play.

Backdoor: A putt which rims the hole before dropping in from the far side.

Backswing: Movement of hands, arms and club away from the ball.

Baffy: A hickory-shafted club, not unlike the modern four wood.

Baseball grip: A two-handed grip in which the fingers of the two hands neither overlap nor inter-lock.

Better-ball: Two players on the same side, each playing their own ball with the lower score of the two counting at each hole.

Birdie: One under par at any one hole.

Bisque: A handicap stroke taken at a hole already played, at the recipient's choice.

Bogey: One over par at any one hole. It is nevertheless an 'Americanism' for in Britain the word bogey used to carry much the same meaning as par today. It was not however quite as demanding since bogey fives were shorter than today's par fives.

Borrow: Slope or undulation of a green.

Brassie: A fairway wood now inclined to be referred to as a two wood.

Bunker: Also known as sand-traps and originated from sheep burrowing for shelter in sand dunes.

Bye: A supplementary game after the main match is over, e.g.: If one player beats another by four holes with three still to play, the bye is played over the remaining holes, usually for a modest sidestake.

Caddie: One who carries a golfer's clubs; he is subject to the same penalties for any breaches of the rules as the player.

Carry: The distance a ball flies before landing.

Casual water: Accumulation of water that is not normally to be found on the course. Applies also to snow and ice.

Chip: A shot to the flag from just off the green, played with an iron club.

Cleek: Hickory-shafted equal of the modern two iron.

Cock: Bending of the wrists on the backswing. Uncocking takes place on the downswing.

Concede: Operates only in match-play when a ball finishes so close to the hole that the opponent does not ask for the putt to be holed. A hole may also be conceded when a player regards himself as certain to lose it.

Course rating: Evaluation of course difficulty, based on its overall yardage.

Croquet putting: Putting, as with a croquet mallet, by swinging the club between the legs. Ruled illegal 1967.

Cup: American expression for the hole in which the flag rests.

Cuppy: A small depression in which the ball may lie.

Cut: Flight of a shot which moves left to right. 'Missing the cut' describes failure to qualify for the last 36 holes of a 72-hole tournament.

Divot: Slice of turf displaced in the playing of a stroke.

Dormie: A golfer is dormie when, in match-play, he is winning by as many holes as there are left to play.

Double eagle: American version of an albatross – three under par at one particular hole.

Draw: Intentional shot which moves slightly from right to left in the air.

Drive: The shot with the driver.

Duck hook: A mis-hit shot which bends sharply right to left.

Duff: Hitting the ground immediately behind the ball.

Eagle: Two under par, for instance a three at a par five hole.

Eclectic: Competition played over a given number of rounds, the player counting his best score at each hole. Also referred to as a Ringer score.

Equity: Decision not covered by the rules.

Face: Area of the clubhead which strikes the ball.

Fade: A stroke which, through the air, moves slightly from left to right.

Fairway: Closely mown area between tee and green.

Feathery: Ball made of stuffed feathers and encased in leather. In common use until mid-19th century.

Feel: A sense of touch, particularly over the shorter shots around the green.

Flat: Swing in which the arc is closer to a horizontal rather than vertical plane.

Flight: Trajectory of the ball.

Fluff: As with the duff, hitting ground behind the ball.

Follow-through: Path of the hands, arms and club after impact.

Fore: Warning shout to other players in danger of being hit by a ball in flight.

Forecaddie: A 'ball spotter' sometimes used in areas of the course where a ball can be lost.

Forward press: Forward movement of the body to release tension before beginning the backswing.

Fourball: Four golfers playing together, each using their own ball. Invariably they then form two teams.

Foursome: Known by Americans as Scotch foursomes. Two players in partnership using one ball, which they hit in turn. One drives off at all the even numbered holes and the other at the odd.

Freeze: Inability to begin the backswing, brought on by nerves. Most common when putting.

Greensome: Similar to foursomes, except that both players drive and then choose which ball to play.

Gross: the number of strokes taken without deduction of handicap.

Ground under repair: A clearly defined area, by club or committee, from which a player may drop his ball clear without penalty.

Half: When, in match-play, opposing sides have the same score at the same hole.

Half shot: Stroke played with a curtailed swing.

Handicap: Receipt of strokes which enables a golfer to equal a course's standard scratch score after reduction from his gross score. (See also *Plus handicap*.)

Hazard: Bunker, pond, river or ditch.

Heavy: Marginally striking the ground behind the ball.

Heel: Head of the club nearest to the shaft.

Hickory: A wooden-shafted club, subsequently replaced by steel shafts.

Honour: The player whose turn it is to drive first.

Hooding: Pronation of the clubhead at the address so as to reduce loft and keep the ball lower to the ground.

Hook: A shot which, for a right-hander, bends left in flight.

Hosel: The socket into which the shaft of the club fits.

In: The second nine holes, inward half or, as Americans sometimes call it, 'the back side'.

Interlocking grip: Entwining of the little finger of the right hand with the first finger of the left – or *vice versa* for a left-hander.

Jigger: A special club for chipping, or bad lies; now virtually obsolete.

Lateral: Lateral water hazards run parallel to the direction of play, it being impractical to drop a ball that is in the hazard behind the point at which it last crossed the margin between the player and the hole.

Lie: Point at which the ball comes to rest.

Line: Intended direction of a stroke.

Links: Seaside course where once the land and sea were linked.

Lip: Edge of the hole.

Loft: designed angle of the clubhead to vary the trajectory of the shot.

Loop: A deviation in the path of the swing, the club apparently 'looping' between the completion of the backswing and the beginning of the downswing.

Lost ball: A ball is lost if it has not been found within five minutes of beginning a search. It can also be declared lost provided another ball is immediately put into play.

Marker: The player responsible for recording another's scorecard.

Mashie: Equivalent of the present-day five iron.

Match-play: Popular form of golf in which holes are won by the player taking the fewer strokes.

Medal-play: Otherwise known as stroke-play. The ball must be holed out at every hole and the player's gross score recorded by his partner or marker.

Metal wood: Misnomer for a club of wooden-headed design, the head in this case being made of metal.

Method: Personal style of play.

Mixed foursomes: When a man and a woman are partners at foursomes.

Municipal course: Known in America as a public course, it is open to anybody on payment of a green fee.

Nap: Grass on greens which grows in a certain direction, making the roll of the ball difficult to judge. Most common in hot climates.

Net: Player's score after he has deducted his handicap allowance.

Niblick: Forerunner of the wedge.

Nineteenth: The first extra, play-off hole if competitors are all-square after 18 holes of match-play. Also refers to the bar in the clubhouse.

Overlapping grip: Also called the Vardon·grip, the little finger of the right hand overlapping the first finger of the left – or *vice versa* for a left-hander.

Out: The first nine holes, outward half or, as Americans sometimes call it, 'the front side'.

Out of bounds: Usually beyond the boundary of the course, which in less obvious cases is marked by white posts. The shot must then be replayed from the original position, counting both the first stroke and a penalty stroke.

Par: A hole measuring up to 250yd (237m) is a par three; one between 251 and 475yd (350m) a par four; one of over 476yd a par five.

Penalty stroke: This may be added to a player's score under the rules.

Pin High: A shot which comes to rest level with the flag, though not necessarily on the green.

Pitch: A lofted approach to the green.

Pitch and run: Stroke played with a less lofted club so that the ball bounces on after landing.

Playing the like: The playing of a stroke which will equal the number of strokes played by the other side.

Playing the odd: The playing of a stroke which will be one more than the number of strokes played by the other side.

Play-off: Method of deciding a tie between two or more players in stroke-play. Usually done now by sudden-death (the first player to win a hole) but in the US Open still over 18 holes.

Plugged ball: A ball embedded in its own pitch mark.

Plus handicap: Handicap allocated to an amateur golfer who regularly scores lower than the standard scratch score.

Pot bunker: Small, relatively deep bunker.

Preferred lies: Emergency procedure when a course is unusually wet, players being allowed to move their ball, though not nearer the hole, without penalty. It does not apply in the rough, other than in casual water.

Pull: A shot left of the target.

Push: A shot right of the target.

Quick: An apparently hurried swing.

Rap: A short, sharp, putting stroke.

Rhythm: A smooth and unhurried swing.

Rub of the green: A lucky or unlucky bounce or deflection.

Run-up: A low chip shot.

Rutting iron: Old fashioned club, now extinct, used for difficult lies.

Sand iron: Broad-soled club used for escaping from bunkers.

Sclaff: Scottish term for hitting the ground behind the ball.

Scratch: A scratch golfer is one who consistently matches the standard scratch score.

Shag bag: Practice-ball bag.

Shank: A mis-hit shot in which the ball is struck with the hosel of the club and flies off at right angles. Also known as a 'socket'.

Short game: Shots around the green.

Singles: A game between two players.

Slice: Shot which curves left to right in flight.

Sole: Bottom of the clubhead.

Spoon: A fairway wood more commonly known these days as a four wood.

Square: Abbreviation of all-square, a match then being level.

Square to square: A method of teaching wherein the clubhead remains at right-angles to the line of play throughout the swing.

Stableford: Popular form of play at club level, under handicap. One point is awarded for a score of one over par, two for par, three for one under, four for two under and five for three under.

Standard scratch score: The number of strokes in which a scratch player is expected to complete the course.

Staying down: Ability not to lift the head before hitting the ball.

Stone dead: A shot which finishes very close to the hole.

Stroke index: Where a handicap golfer receives his handicap strokes, either against another player or against the card.

Stymie: Until 1951, when it was outlawed, the stymie was very much a part of match-play. A ball lying between the hole and an opponent's ball on the green could be left. This was called 'laying a stymie'.

Sway: Lateral movement of the head and body during the swing.

Swing weight: Weight of the club head felt by the golfer when swinging the club; adjustable according to individual preference.

Take away: The first movement of hands, arms and club away from the ball.

Tempo: As with rhythm, a smooth and unhurried swing.

Temporary green: Mostly used in winter and then only in an emergency to save a normal green from damage.

Texas wedge: Description of a stroke played with the putter from off the green.

Thin: A slight mis-hit resulting from the leading edge of the sole of the club hitting the ball.

Threeball: Contested between three players, each in opposition to the other two.

Threesome: Two players in partnership, using one ball as in foursomes, against a single player with his own ball.

Through the green: Everywhere on the course except on the tee or the green of the hole being played.

Tight course: One on which it can be punishing to miss narrow fairways because of heavy rough or thick vegetation.

Toe: Part of the club face furthest from the shaft.

Top: Mis-hit which catches the top of the ball.

Trap: American expression for bunker.

Trouble: Another word for rough, bunkers etc.

Twitch: Otherwise known as the 'yips'; a nervous, involuntary putting stroke near to the hole. More common among those of advancing years.

Up: A golfer is up when he has won more holes than his opponent.

Upright: A swing in which the arc is closer to a vertical rather than horizontal plane.

Water hazard: Lake, pond, river, ditch, or sea.

Wedge: A lofted club, useful for getting out of deep rough and also for lofted approach shots to the green.

Wry neck: Club in which the head is aligned slightly behind the shaft; most common in putters.

INDEX